DOING
EMOTION

DOING
EMOTION

Rhetoric, Writing, Teaching

LAURA R. MICCICHE

Foreword by
RICHARD E. MILLER

Boynton/Cook Publishers
HEINEMANN
Portsmouth, NH

Boynton/Cook Publishers, Inc.
A subsidiary of Reed Elsevier Inc.
361 Hanover Street
Portsmouth, NH 03801–3912
www.boyntoncook.com

Offices and agents throughout the world

The author and publisher wish to thank those who have generously given permission to reprint borrowed material:

Excerpts from Chapter Four originally appeared in "More Than a Feeling: Disappointment and WPA Work" from *College English* 64, March 2002. Copyright © 2002 by the National Council of Teachers of English. Reprinted with permission

Library of Congress Cataloging-in-Publication Data
Micciche, Laura R.
    Doing emotion : rhetoric, writing, teaching / Laura Micciche.
        p. cm.
    Includes bibliographical references and index.
    ISBN-13: 978-0-325-01099-1
    ISBN-10: 0-325-01099-4
    1. English language—Rhetoric—Study and teaching (Higher)—Psychological aspects. 2. Report writing—Study and teaching (Higher)—Psychological aspects. 3. College students—Psychology. 4. Language and emotions. I. Title

PE1404.M53 2007
808'.0420711—dc22   2007024170

Editor: Charles I. Schuster
Production service: bookworks publishing services, Lisa S. Garboski
Production coordinator: Lynne Costa
Cover design: Night & Day Design
Typesetter: Valerie Levy / Drawing Board Studios
Manufacturing: Jamie Carter

Printed in the United States of America on acid-free paper
11   10   09   08   07   VP   1   2   3   4   5

For
Mary Louise Micciche, 1917–2002
Gary and Giovanni

Contents

Foreword

As I was preparing this foreword, the news broke about the campus massacre at Virginia Tech. Thirty-three dead. Twenty-nine wounded. One more chapter in America's uniquely awful history of education and violence. And in the days that have followed, the media have sought out all available images of grief, running on an endless loop the video Seung-Hui Cho made to ensure that he lived on in the minds of those who survived his rampage. And, as always, questions have proliferated, debates raged: Why was there a delay in responding to the initial act of violence? Why hadn't anyone picked up on all the warning signs, now so obvious in retrospect? Why was someone with a history of mental illness able to purchase firearms?

When the camera crews and journalists pack up and move on to the next big story, the nation won't be any closer to understanding how it is that things can go so wrong in places committed to education. A young man with a grudge, a fathomless pain, the by-now-predictable outcome. The focus always tight on the individual: the enraged young man, the grieving X, the betrayed Y, the outraged Z. When we have gone through the full cycle of this analysis, we'll be back where we started, ready to start up again as the occasion demands. And that is the only certainty: this will happen again.

For those dissatisfied with analyses of higher education that never rise above the personal experience of individuals—be those individuals heroic teachers, troubled students, or disheartened administrators, Laura Micciche offers an alternate approach for reading and responding to the interpersonal dynamics that shape every pedagogical exchange. With her opening assessment that "Tendencies to think of emotions as *only* personally experienced and felt are simply not adequate to describe how emotions take form and are coded as appropriate or inappropriate within communities," Micciche wrests both the experience and the concept of emotion from a rhetorical and pedagogical tradition that has been content to promote the well-made argument as the bedrock of the language arts. In this tradition, Reason has long been depicted as the universal force that draws us all together through the community-building activities of argumentation, persuasion, and deliberation; emotion, by contrast, is figured as the countervailing force, alternately merely a private possession and the fuel that burns brightest when the mob is on the move.

By asking her readers to see emotion as a binding force—as that which makes linguistic and rhetorical exchanges "sticky"— Micciche encourages us to acknowledge that emotions are not simply "in here," but also "out there," simultaneously created by and preceding us all. In so doing, she opens up for re-examination the form and function of those twin narratives that have defined the field of rhetoric and composition—teaching as liberatory and teaching as the sad slog through the dungeons of despair. She also provides the occasion for re-thinking the role the emotions play in the composing process beyond serving as the stamp that establishes an experience as deep and authentic. (I wept. I was outraged. I laughed. I. I. I.) What this perspectival shift away from the emoting *I* makes possible is the thought that change comes about not by focusing on individuals in isolation, but on individuals in relation to one another, individuals in context. What Micciche advises, in short, is that we think of rhetoric not as something that one person *does* to another, but rather as a way of binding individuals together through language.

"How do we teach something that happens *in relation*?" Micciche asks early on, before turning her attention to responding to this challenge. In so doing, she demonstrates that the recent turn in scholarship towards the emotions does not necessitate a turn away from considering either the political potential or the political consequences of rhetorical practice. Rather, Micciche demonstrates that focusing on emotion casts the challenges that writing teachers and administrators face today in an entirely new light. That the emotional realities of teaching have changed significantly over the past decade is undeniable; *Doing Emotion* provides much needed guidance both on understanding these changes and on imagining a responsive pedagogy for these emotionally fraught times—a pedagogy grounded not in fear but in hope for better times.

Richard E. Miller
Rutgers University

Preface: Roots and Limbs

I believe this book began to take form in my grandmother's kitchen some thirty-odd years ago. In there, the boiling pots of pasta mixed with thick layers of cigarette smoke, the smell of booze, and the booming voice of Grandma Micciche. Her every word seemed to emerge from a deep well of emotion, even if those words were as mundane as "I damn near burned my finger!" There was such conviction in her performative displays of emotion, which careened from one extreme to another, inciting a range of conflicting responses from those around her: from sheer delight and ecstatic pleasure to foreboding and fear. Grandma was a passionate woman —loud, loving, sweet, and fearsome; all of these intertwined and embodied.

Those early memories of Grandma have stuck with me, and over time I've come to think of her emotional excess as more than an expression of feeling or a personality trait. That excess was also her "terministic screen," to borrow from Kenneth Burke, by which she made sense of and participated in the world. It was the organizing principle from which other things evolved. When disappointed or flustered, she proclaimed, "Well, shit the bed!" as if to say, there's no stopping the shit-flow—may as well adapt to things as they are. In another scatological phrase, Grandma announced, after stymied by a series of obstacles, "Life's a shit sandwich, and every day's another bite." In fact, these phrases adhered so completely to Grandma's persona that her children created a milestone birthday cake for her embossed with "Shit the bed, you're 60!"

I could read these phrases as fatalistic proclamations having something to do with working-class perspectives and experiences, but I choose not to. Instead, I read them as creative, emotioned assessments of the everyday that do a lot of *work* in terms of communication. These are funny phrases that I loved, still love, for their vividness (to put it mildly!) as well as for their direct, unapologetic raunchiness. They are phrases that characterize Grandma's irreverent way of using emotion and humor in order to present her read on the world, to process daily life through an uncluttered and incautious frame of reference. Emotion was crucial to how Grandma came to know things, to develop connections and attachments to others, and to function in the world. She used language to perform and embody emotion, by which I mean that she did not tell us how she felt via meta-commentary, for she didn't seem to need narratives of personal feeling as a way to transmit emotion or express care; instead, she embodied feeling through performances of the everyday—both linguistic and bodily-based.

I write this knowing that I never thought any of these things when I was a child, on those Sunday afternoons my family spent at Grandma's house, eating and watching football and horsing around. I see that time in my life as the seedling for this project—the beginning of a line of thought about emotion as a lived, embodied concept. My thinking has evolved from that initial experience, absorbing along the way other reference points, including, perhaps idiosyncratically, the literature of Fyodor Dostoevsky, which first altered my orientation to reading when I was an adolescent, then again while an undergraduate enrolled in a Dostoevsky and Ingmar Bergman course, and then again, and differently, when teaching an undergraduate course on Dostoevsky's novels. The psychological intensity of his worlds, including the density of emotion as embodied by characters, was spellbinding to me. It's not that the characters were emotional *only* in the way that term is often understood: sappy, self-indulgent, and irrational (although many of his characters can be aptly described this way, I'd argue that none can be wholly encapsulated by these representations of *being emotional*). Rather, the characters' ways of seeing the world and attaching to or detaching from others were represented with arduous complexity and faithfulness to felt experience as a guiding force for decision-making, action, and inaction. Raskolnikov's decision in *Crime and Punishment* to transgress morality in order to serve a higher purpose emerges from his belief that he is one of the unusual few entitled to "step over" morality in the name of a better future. Thus, his ultimately flawed but painstakingly elaborate plan to murder an old pawnbroker—a "vermin" on society, from his perspective—evolved from an emotional investment and faithful belief in the need for a universe organized by a kind of Napoleonic moral code.

What I learned from Dostoevsky's work is that emotion adheres to morality, judgment, belief, and ethics. It is central to how we attach ourselves to concepts and the actions and decisions that evolve from them. From my current perspective, I responded to Dostoevsky's depiction of emotions as performative insofar as they are expressions involving and animating the body as well as sociocultural scripts of one sort or another. Framing emotion as a performative, as I do in this book, is the result of working through the theoretical contexts of feminist rhetorical theories and performance studies, among other interdisciplinary projects, in order to carry out "concept undoing," a necessary step toward concept-building. I think such reconstruction is especially important in composition studies, in which the "emotional appeal," as delineated through Aristotle's psychology of emotions, frequently operates as tacit shorthand for manipulation, excess, and irrationality—a disreputable source about which we should remain suspect. As scholars in the field have begun to insist, and as this book seeks to demonstrate, rethinking emotion beyond the emotional appeal as traditionally understood leads to exciting, innovative pedagogical methods as well as to reinvigorated studies of emotion as a rhetoric of bodies and beliefs in motion.

I hope the eclectic frames of reference that I bring to the study of emotion as a rhetorical concept will appeal to a broad audience, including composition teachers, rhetorical theorists, and those interested in questions of culture and identity. With composition teachers in mind, I have developed exercises for the classroom aimed at putting emotion into play so as to reveal its relational, embodied qualities. My motivation is twofold. Firstly, bored and disappointed by approaches to emotion that cast it as an always suspect, usually fallacious feature of persuasive discourse, I wanted new ideas to inform and re-energize my own teaching practices in first-year writing classes and beyond. I have a hunch that other teachers have likewise grown weary of the usual depiction of emotion as one of rhetoric's dispossessed offspring. If I'm right, the performative classroom exercises described in Chapter Three may function as grounds from which to improvise other practices and to offer possibilities for how to go live with emotion in the classroom. Secondly, I believe that we can help sharpen students' reading, writing, and thinking skills by enacting emotion in the classroom through creative practices. This belief is based on the assumption that when we attempt to approximate experience through performance, we come to know experience (and identity) differently, often more attentively and intimately than we might otherwise. There's untapped potential, I argue, for recognizing rhetoric via performative pedagogies that seek to bring alive seemingly remote, obscure, and/or ineffable concepts.

For rhetorical theorists, I offer a revisionist theory of emotion that borrows from and builds on contemporary theories, most of which put a premium on emotion as a social act that shapes and is shaped by social norms, conventions, and acts of resistance. As such, *Doing Emotion* contributes to ongoing efforts to seize upon rhetoric's continuing relevance to what we do in composition studies and, more generally, to evolving ideas about the business of using language. To those interested in questions of culture and identity, I provide examples of emotion perception, interpretation, and expression as culturally specific acts. These acts shape identity and function as grounds for developing attachments to people and things. Admitting emotion into understandings of cultural and identity formations especially deepens our commitment to exploring the interplay of differences in our classrooms and university experiences as well as in our scholarship.

Most of all, I hope this book creates more questions than it answers. This effect would certainly mirror my composing process, which lurched forward, lost footing, backtracked, and began anew after uncovering, through writing and researching, new questions to animate and alter my movement throughout this book.

Acknowledgments

Thanks to

. . . Chuck Schuster for saying, "There's a monograph in here," when I needed to hear that. I'm grateful for Chuck's editing suggestions, which revealed to me some of my unconscious and unproductive writing habits.

. . . The editorial staff at Boynton/Cook for such careful handling of my manuscript and superb guidance throughout the process.

. . . The anonymous reviewer, whose encouraging comments gave me a second wind and whose thoughts on problems with an earlier version of Chapter Two helped me rethink my goal.

. . . Jeanne Gunner and Eileen Schell for responding so affirmatively and critically to an early draft of Chapter Four, the thinking in which marks one beginning of this book.

. . . Wendy Sharer and Michelle Gibson for early generative feedback on my lousy first drafts. Seriously, I'm grateful and a little embarrassed. And later, Jonathan Alexander, Russel Durst, and Lucy Schultz for careful readings that saw the potential in my early, still messy (but not as lousy) draft. Later still, Gary Weissman for sensitive, close readings that helped me untangle my sentences.

. . . Dale Jacobs, Alice Gillam, and Eve Wiederhold for conversations over the years that triggered ideas and kept me on track, even if they didn't realize it.

. . . The University of Cincinnati Department of English and Comparative Literature for generous release time from teaching to work on this book. Lee Person for supporting my ongoing research and accommodating my requests for scheduling flexibility. The University of Cincinnati Taft Center Summer Research grant in 2005 for support of this book, which made it possible for me to write steadily throughout the summer.

. . . The graduate students in Critical Writing for English Studies during spring 2006, especially Rachel Zlatkin, who got me thinking about performativity and embodiment before I knew these ideas would figure into this book.

. . . My colleagues and students—Richard Bullock, Gretchen Flesher Moon, Gregory Glau, Vicki Holmsten, Christina McDonald, and Bill Thelin; Heather Hughes, Arielle McCoy, and Stephanie Spiker—for granting me permission to quote their words in here. *College English* and NCTE for permission to reprint a slightly revised version of "More than a Feeling: Disappointment and WPA Work" (March 2002) as Chapter Four and to *JAC* for permission to reprint one section of "Emotion, Ethics, and Rhetorical Action" (2005).

. . . Those feline wonders for daily consistency mixed with good doses of surprise and silliness.

. . . My family—parents, bro, in-laws—for suspending disbelief and supporting my efforts through acts of generosity: babysitting, visits, dinners, and euchre.

. . . My two Gs for everything, especially the toys, the books, the outside play, the laughs, the irrepressible emotion, and the incredible, insistent wonder of everything.

Introduction:
Emotion as a Category of Analysis

In academic as well as popular culture, emotions raise suspicion because they are said to cloud judgment and manipulate reason. Indeed, emotion is regularly cast as reason's spoiler, by everyone from Nietzsche to Donald Trump. Yet this view hardly begins to capture the nuanced ways in which emotion contributes to meaning-making, judgment formation, and communication. My reading of emotion as a valuable rhetorical resource—that is, as central to how we become invested in people, ideas, structures, and objects—seeks to make an intervention in how the elements of rhetoric are typically described in composition studies. In relying primarily on classical formulations of rhetoric that privilege reason, compositionists tend to either neglect or underestimate emotion's presence in the process of meaning-making, as do many writing textbooks that describe Aristotle's pathetic appeal. We treat emotion as additive to meaningful discourse at a cost, for emotion suffuses everything from political arguments to social movements to everyday acts of communication and understanding. Without a framework for understanding emotion's legitimate role in the making of meaning and in the creation of value in our culture, we impoverish our own and our students' understanding of how we come to orient ourselves to one another and to the world around us.

In fact, I argue that to best understand emotion's role in binding the social body together (and tearing it apart), we need to grasp emotion as a category of analysis. Rather than characterize emotion exclusively as a reaction to a situation or a tool used to create a reaction in an audience, we need to shift our thinking to examine how emotion is part of the "stickiness" that generates attachments to others, to world-views, and to a whole array of sources and objects. The distinction to press here is between the study of *emoting*, or the expression of feeling, and that of *rhetorics of emotion*, or emotion as a performative that produces effects. To speak of emotion as performative is to foreground the idea that emotions are enacted and embodied in the social world. It is also to posit emotions as

1

produced between people and between people and things. That is, we *do* emotions—they don't simply happen to us. This claim suggests that studying rhetorics of emotion requires a total rethinking of how to describe, identify, and apply the Aristotelian emotional appeal. As I discuss more fully in Chapter Three, analyzing rhetorics of emotion requires attention to extralinguistic features around the world of a text—features, often considered ineffable, such as body language, gesture, and movement—because these elements are entry points to understanding emotion as an embodied performative, as that which exceeds and shapes our connection to textuality.

The consequences of rhetorics of emotion, understood in the way just described, are as yet relatively unexamined in composition studies. This absence is understandable given the centrality of logos to establishing composition's research agenda. As scholars such as James Berlin (1987), Lester Faigley (1993), and Maureen Daly Goggin (2000) have explained, the rise of qualitative and descriptive research methods during the 1970s and 1980s made possible systematic studies of writing processes. Moving beyond experimental or idiosyncratic studies of writing skills, these studies promised to strengthen composition's status as a legitimate field by introducing research methods that produced hard, empirical evidence about teaching writing. This approach became the object of critique as social and political perspectives on writing processes began to emerge in the late 1980s and early 1990s (see Ede 2004, especially Chapter Three). In a different vein, the recovery of ancient rhetorics as vital resources for the teaching of writing offered another logos-centered boost to the field's research agenda. By demonstrating that epistemological frameworks for teaching writing have a basis in ancient articulations of rhetoric, scholars carved out an intellectual tradition lending credibility to writing as a rhetorical activity.

The use of empirical research methods and the revitalization of ancient rhetorical practice and theory for contemporary audiences represent different moments in the development of Composition Studies. Now that the field has attained disciplinary status—although teaching writing continues to be identified as service rather than intellectual work—it is timely to consider what narrative threads within composition's story remain unattended to as a result of logos-heavy explanations. Emotion's pedagogical and rhetorical potential is one such thread. Reassessing emotion in light of current interdisciplinary projects moves us from a limited model of emotion as an audience-centric tool to an expansive model in which emotion is an analytical, rhetorical, and performative *act*. Shifting our thinking in this way has the capacity to alter depictions of composition studies as more than the sum of its history, scholarship, and evolved practices. The field's subjectivity is also constituted by affective stances on writing, rhetoric, pedagogy, and the many surrounding issues related to each. These stances are perhaps more aptly described as positioning tools, or the means by which compositionists have collectively generated an ethos that sticks to the field, calling to mind, for instance, frequent representations of it as democratic, inclusive, and friendly. In other words, key claims in composition studies emerge from emotioned ways of seeing our work no less than they do from intellectual and historical traditions. I use the term *emotioned* here and elsewhere to designate the active role that writers in the field take in crafting pedagogical practices and theories. This includes narratives of composition's development, motivated by, grounded in, and/or reflective of emotional investments in how things ought to be, although these investments are not regularly acknowledged in such terms.

And no wonder. One of the problems associated with positioning emotion as a category of analysis is the tendency within intellectual as well as popular thought to collapse emotion with all things feminine, a marker that, at least in the history of academic discourse, has signaled a tendency to be weak, shallow, petty, vain, and narcissistic. Emotion, much like rhetoric, has been denoted as having a "mere" quality. To say that an argument is "merely" emotive is tantamount to saying it is not representative, but instead personal and idiosyncratic; not thoughtful, but solely reliant on opinion, which academics are more than ready to cast as suspicious, often with good reason. What we do when we argue or persuade, students' remarks in class often remind me, is construct a rational position *after* sifting through emotional responses. Calm, cool, and collected—the three Cs of argument. Yet, I wonder, isn't the very process of deliberation already an emotioned one, already bound up with attachments we have to a way of seeing or conceptualizing an issue? In other words, how we think about what constitutes evidence and grounds for an argument—indeed, how we come to decide that an issue deserves to be "argued"—is already shaped by our emotional investments in how things ought to be.

In addition, my students' comments remind me that the reason-emotion binary obscures the fuzzy distinctions between these concepts. So, for instance, we forget to know that it is possible to be calm while emoting or to be righteous while cloaking oneself in the guise of reason. Or we forget that it is possible to use "reasonable" discourse while expressing prejudicial rhetoric possessed by a single way of seeing an issue or problem, a chosen blindness to "truth" usually associated with overly emotional discourse. Likewise, surely we can show emotion, perhaps especially empathy, while "reasonably" weighing competing ideas in search of a solution. Whose life, whose thinking, whose writing is divisible into moments characterized by "reason" and "emotion" in a clean, uncontaminated—indeed, clinical—way?

For me, then, a question to which I have continually returned while thinking about emotion as a category of analysis is the following: What really is at stake in positioning emotion as outside efforts to reason, communicate, and act meaningfully? Repeatedly I find myself face-to-face with emotion's metonym: the hysterical woman whose mysteries and absences have been so thoroughly fetishized in Freudian psychoanalysis. In fact, feminized views of emotion tend not only to associate women with emotion and its perceived excesses but also to locate emotion *in* the female; she herself is often designated as the site of emoting and thus of irrationality and excess. Charlotte Perkins Gilman (1892/2001) eerily represents this figure in her classic story, "The Yellow Wallpaper." The narrator, suffering from postpartum depression, has been isolated by her physician husband John as a condition of the "rest cure," a precaution against her tendency to over-emote. Internalizing his privileging of rationality and anything "put down in figures" (Gilman 1892/2001, 265), the narrator attempts to keep her emotions in check: "I get unreasonably angry with John sometimes. I'm sure I never used to be so sensitive. I think it is due to this nervous condition" (ibid., 265). Self-control is a key ingredient in John's view of normal, appropriate behavior, so the narrator takes "pains to control myself—before him at least, and that makes me very tired" (ibid., 265). John is the rational figure who can't understand faith or superstition, while the narrator embodies her "nervous condition," further irritating it by her desire to write, which John sees as dangerous because of writing's capacity to unearth emotions better left buried. "He says that with my imaginative power and habit of story making, a nervous weakness like mine is sure to lead to all manner of excited fancies, and that I ought to use my will and good sense to check the tendency. So I try" (ibid., 267). Fragile, prone to fantasy and exaggeration, resistant to the very treatment that promises to "cure" what ails her, the narrator indeed embodies emotional excess, a condition so dangerous that it requires isolation from the rest of the world and from any form of expression that might further trigger unwieldy emotions.

In Gilman's story, the narrator sees women behind the yellow wallpaper struggling to get out; they "creep" beneath the surface of the seemingly ordinary, though sickly and dreary, yellow wallpaper. Like these women struggling just beneath the surface, feminist literary critics, especially those writing during the late 1980s and early 1990s, struggled to unbind themselves from the strictures of academic discourse that presumed a disembodied writer. The depersonalized academic voice as a learned ethos of the true scholar informs the much-celebrated attempt by Jane Tompkins in "Me and My Shadow" (1991) to make room for the embodied critic. She tells us that she's been "hiding a part of [her]self for a long time" because "there was no place for this person in literary criticism" (Tompkins 1991, 1083). The pretense of objectivity in academic discourse produces what she calls the "authority effect" (ibid., 1085), which effectively ignores "the human frailty of the speaker, his body, his emotions, his history; the moment of intercourse with the reader—acknowledgment of the other person's presence, feelings, needs. This 'authoritative' language speaks as though the other person weren't there" (ibid., 1085). Tompkins' formulation of the problem with literary theory and its consequences rests on her experience as a critic. For her, disembodied writing exacts too high a cost as it demands that she leave behind her self, her body, her material conditions, and her personal connection to language and story.

Tompkins' essay makes apparent how emotion (along with the personal and the body) has been schooled out of academic discourse. This is precisely why it's shocking to read her explosion of feeling near the end of the piece:

> Is the molten lava of millennia of hatred boiling below the surface of every essay, every book, every syllabus, every newsletter, every little magazine? I imagine that I can open the front of my stomach like a door, reach in, and pluck from memory the rooted sorrow, pull it out, root and branch. But where, or rather, who, would I be then? I am attached to this rage. It is a source of identity for me. (ibid., 1091)

With her emotions in full view, and her admission of that most unfeminine of other-directed emotions right there in front of us—rage—Tompkins forces herself upon us, making a spectacle of herself as no self-respecting woman should. Emotion's appearance in Tompkins' essay calls into question the assumptions built into literary criticism that tacitly guide what we think of as critical writing, making visible the normalized value system that is largely dependent on the evacuation of emotion.

Tompkins ends up producing a piece of criticism in which she is very much present. Even her bodily functions make an appearance. As she writes what began as a response to an essay by Ellen Messer-Davidow, Tompkins tells us that she wishes to do literary criticism in a way that doesn't try to "beat the other person down," but she doesn't know how to write differently. Most importantly, she doesn't know how to enter the debate "without leaving everything else behind—the birds outside my window, my grief over Janice [a colleague who committed suicide], just myself as a person sitting here in stockinged feet, a little bit chilly because the windows are open, and thinking about going to the bathroom. But not going yet" (ibid., 1083). This moment in the essay puts her self, her feelings, her situation, her body on display, reminding us, as did Virginia Woolf in *A Room of One's Own*, that writing is made possible by a whole set of material realities, not the least of which is that we have bodies and feelings that make a difference when it comes to how and why we put words on the page. Tompkins' essay illustrates that the cultural production of emotion is sanctioned and penalized in distinct ways, varies according to context and community, and has tangible consequences affecting one's sense of self and purpose.

As a result, then, of historical processes that have constructed emotion as dangerous and untrustworthy, emotion has been the object of a large-scale dismissal, rendering invisible its principal work on how we come to orient ourselves to the world, including how we develop, interpret, and analyze our own investments in the things we value through complex social and cultural rituals and norms. In other words, what gets mystified in traditional views of emotion is the extent to which emotion expression and perception are mediated rather than natural responses to a situation. Sara Ahmed (2004), author of *The Cultural Politics of Emotion*, sharpens this point when she writes,

> [E]motions are what move us, and how we are moved involves interpretations of sensations and feelings not only in the sense that we interpret what we feel, but also in that what we feel might be dependent on past interpretations that are not necessarily made by us, but that come before us. Focusing on emotions as mediated rather than immediate reminds us that knowledge cannot be separated from the bodily world of feeling and sensation [...]. (Ahmed 2004, 171)

In this formulation, emotion is always bound up with knowledge, what is thought rather than exclusively felt. This idea undermines the familiar binary that keeps reason and emotion in check, a binary that seems to me unnecessarily limiting and, worse, inaccurate when it comes to assessing, theorizing, and teaching the functions and uses of rhetoric. Instead, by demonstrating that emotion is part of what makes ideas adhere, generating investments and attachments that get recognized as positions and/or perspectives, this study challenges longstanding views of emotion as unreasonable, as a mark of feminine excess, and as exclusively personal. Tendencies to think of emotions as *only* personally experienced and felt are simply not adequate to describe how emotions take form and are coded as appropriate or inappropriate within communities. Binding emotion to the personal ignores emotion's contribution to everyday acts of communication; it also seriously diminishes the place of emotion in rhetorical studies.

For too long emotion has stood for subjugated knowledge, by functioning as analog to women, opinion, the personal, and the body. My use of emotion as a key term is intended as both a recuperation of a much neglected, under-theorized facet of rhetorical theory, at least in the context of composition discourse, and as a direct challenge to the disparagement of emotion in popular and intellectual culture. To figure emotion as a critical term that can illuminate perspectives on the content of intellectual work in new, refreshed ways—similar to how gendered, sexed, and raced analyses, for instance, have re-excavated the landscape of composition studies—is to take seriously the work that emotions do in the context of disciplinary formation, teaching, and administering writing. My larger goal, then, is to demonstrate that emotions perform and embody meanings we take for granted or entirely fail to acknowledge, and that becoming aware of emotion as a legitimate rhetoric promises to revitalize theory and practice in composition studies. We are overdue for muddying the longstanding boundary between reason and emotion and learning to recognize that this binary is a disabling fiction that serves masculinized, clichéd, and far too categorical views of knowledge, discourse, and action.

Chapters At a Glance

I cannot write about emotion as a category of analysis, as a rhetorical and theoretical concept, without addressing the expectations that inform most people's thinking about emotion as an expression of feeling. In composition studies emotion and the emotional appeal most often signify *emoting*, an expression of feeling that speaks from and about the self. But the conception of emotion that informs this book—emotion as part of what makes meanings stick, as integral to rhetorical action—poses a very different model for doing what might be called *emotion analysis*. To contextualize and enlarge this point, Chapter One describes why *emotion*, rather than *feeling* or *affect*, is my key term, and details the characteristics of my working definition of emotion. This definition holds that emotion is experienced between people within a particular context (and so resides both *in* people and *in* culture) and that emotion is an expression, experience, and perception mediated by language, body, and culture. This chapter also addresses why emotion studies are proliferating across the disciplines at this particular moment, leading to a consideration of why and how emotion matters to composition studies as well as to composition teachers.

Chapter Two focuses on emotioned discourse as a core ingredient of composition's identity and mission. Although emotion is always already a part of knowledge-construction, what is absent in composition studies are the tools for recognizing its presence in so-called rational discourse. Chapter Two employs Ahmed's term *stickiness*, which refers to the "accumulation of affective value" that binds emotions with objects and surfaces. This concept helps me to explore how frequently used identity metaphors in composition discourse involve a sticky transference of affect that adheres to notions of the field, composition teachers, and composition courses. The resulting emotional subjection—emergent from metaphors linking composition and its teachers to whores, maids, and the proletariat, among other oppressed figures—*sticks* and demonstrates that composition's identity metaphors exceed description of a status location. They indicate an affective disposition that sticks to the field and those associated with it, creating paradoxical opportunities for change in the process. In the final section of this chapter, I explore the dynamic between persistent metaphors of subordination in composition discourse and changed realities for writing teachers. Using Wendy Brown's (1995) notion of "wounded attachments," I argue that the habituated self-presentation as subordinate offers no real place from which to move the field forward; rather, it amplifies what we already know but fails to map out new meanings through which composition might come to construct alternative, forward-looking identifications. Also, feelings of dispossession and hurt get bound together with those who teach writing courses and with the field itself, enabling the continued blurring of teacher/course with specialist/field—these categories become interlaced through an overarching emotional disposition that gets expressed through metaphor.

The rest of my argument unfolds in a similar fashion, with subsequent chapters modeling how to configure the emotional appeal as more than a tool for emoting or getting others to emote. In Chapter Three, "Emotion Performed and Embodied in the Writing Classroom," I sketch several pedagogical exercises for teaching emotion as an embodied performative. Drawing from research in performance studies, I argue that teaching methods using movement and play can effectively illuminate emotion as produced *between* people, as always entailing a culturally situated performance, thus generating more complexity and dimension around rhetorics of emotion than does a purely textual orientation. This chapter is provisional in nature, for rather than presenting an ethnography of classroom experience or describing an already tested set of assignments, I position past teaching experiences as windows through which to review and rethink my approach to (not) teaching emotion as a rhetorical concept. To be sure, I am in good company as one who has not taught students how to understand and deploy emotion critically and rhetorically; current research in English and education overwhelmingly positions emotion as an analytic for assessing working conditions and teacherly identity, not as a teachable concept that students may learn how to register and use differently. My attempt to begin this conversation is largely focused on the value of reconceiving emotion through extralinguistic, inventive means, an approach with a surprising surplus of untapped potential.

Moving from the classroom to the site of writing program administration, Chapter Four, "Disappointment and WPA Work," addresses the climate of disappointment that I argue characterizes writing program administration (WPA) discourse. I focus on the limitations imposed by the affective experience of disappointment and the strategic ways in which WPAs use disappointment as a framework for effecting change, however compromised and tempered it may be. By portraying disappointment as an emotion through which we can analyze work practices, this chapter argues that shared emotioned experience reveals insights that both include and go beyond private expressions of emotion. Thus, I argue that rather than continuing to talk primarily among ourselves about the troubling working conditions for most WPAs, compositionists must begin to contribute to the larger dialogue on administration and to articulate WPA's reality to a wider audience, those very people who have some stake in how a department organizes, defines, and evaluates its work.

In the following interchapter, "Experience and Emotion," I describe a discussion strand that appeared on WPA-L after the initial publication of Chapter Four in *College English* (Micciche, 2002). The essay's publication prompted an extended public discussion on the list, in which emotional experience emerged as an authorizing discourse determining whether people identify what I name a "climate of disappointment" in English broadly and WPA specifically. I reflect on this discussion and the juggernaut of emotion and experience in order to probe further the tight weave between identity and emotion and, shifting contexts, to think about the risks posed by making emotion an explicit term of study and thought in classrooms, where experience, presented as an emotional truth, threatens to undo and negate critical thought. Although this issue comes up briefly in Chapter Three, I use this interchapter to go into more depth about experience as an authenticating, and sometimes tyrannical, discourse fueled by emotion. I am interested in how scholars and writing teachers can cultivate rigor and critical thought around emotion that, despite complications, does not rule out experience and the body but rather makes both a site of contestation and productive tension.

My concluding chapter argues that asking what emotions *do*, rather than what they are or where we might locate them, is a central question for reinserting rhetoric into our field's continuing engagement with emotion. To move our thinking toward this question, I advocate practicing *wild mind*, a methodology described by environmental theorist Paul Wapner (2003) as a means for thinking anew about any idea or concept. Wapner explains that "wild mind means a commitment to freeing our own intellect and exploring where our thoughts take us rather than worrying about replicating the ideas of others" (20). Such liberatory thinking is what we need to refresh our understanding and application of emotion in relation to writing and rhetoric; it is a way of opening possibility where for so long we have faced seemingly foregone conclusions.

Chapter One

On Terms and Context

*We are called on to make emotion a critical category—an occasion
for interrogation—rather than a comforting warrant for truth and
authenticity.*

Lynn Worsham, "Afterword"

In Book 2 of *On Rhetoric*, Aristotle defines the emotions as "those
things through which, by undergoing change, people come to differ
in their judgments . . ." (Aristole trans. 1991, 121). As suggested by his
emphasis on judgment—a motived assessment that needs a self in relation to others—emotion is a thoroughly social concept for Aristotle.
When speaking of indignation, for example, he speculates that "if
being indignant is being distressed at the evidence of unworthy success, it is clear, first of all, that it is not possible to be indignant at all
good things [that others acquire or possess]" (ibid., 156). Emotion,
here indignation, is experienced *in relation*, between people within a
particular context. Aristotle's configuration of emotion, then, is thoroughly rhetorical because he locates the meaning of emotion in the
context of social life, where people tacitly agree upon what counts
as indignation or any other emotion. That is, only through collective, implicit assent in communal life does emotion have meaning,
for here is where identification of emotion is ascribed to expression
and perception, which comes to stand for what we have agreed to
interpret as, following the foregoing example, *indignation*. There is no
natural biological entity objectively known as indignation.[1]

By linking emotion to change and judgment, Aristotle evokes emotion's function as an action, a tool for *doing*. In addition, using a contemporary screen, we glean from Aristotle that emotion is processed through language, through the body (gesture and voice are technologies of emotion for Aristotle), and through intention. The processed components resist familiar characterizations of emotion as a natural form of expression, an unmediated display of feeling that is truly "from the heart." That emotions are embodied—expressed by, experienced, and perceived through a body located in time, space, and culture—is by no means an indication that they are therefore natural. "Embodying the emotions also involves theoretically situating them in the social body such that one can examine how emotional discourses are formed by and in the shapes of the ecologies and political economies in which they arise" (Abu-Lughod and Lutz 1990, 13). Emotions form an economy of relations among people and within culture; they are produced by what Sara Ahmed calls "effects of circulation" (Ahmed 2004, 8).

We see examples of this every day, but to home in on a current one, let's look at President Bush's February 2004 call for a constitutional amendment to "protect" marriage. In his speech delivered at the Roosevelt Room in the White House, he warns, "If we are to prevent the meaning of marriage from being changed forever, our nation must enact a constitutional amendment to protect marriage in America. Decisive and democratic action is needed, because attempts to redefine marriage in a single state or city could have serious consequences throughout the country" (Bush 2006). Here and elsewhere, Bush evokes fear that marriage will become irrevocably different, that marriage as we know it is under threat and thereby needs protection. He also seeks to generate anger about the "serious consequences" sure to be elicited by a changed concept of marriage and to stir up pride as he calls for "democratic action," a deeply hopeful tool for change in the U.S. There is an effort in this speech to circulate emotions of fear and pride among the American people, to create an orientation to the issue that is endorsed by the most powerful office in the country.

Although we might be tempted to categorize Bush's emotioned rhetoric as an example of the marriage between emotion and manipulation, thus neglecting to take seriously the intended rhetorical effects of his speech, I want to suggest that there is something more complex sought after in Bush's highly charged framing of the issues. For one thing, his rhetoric reveals that there is a *need* to produce emotioned worries around marriage because most people are not already equipped with the belief that marriage needs protection, that it is an institution "under threat" requiring a preemptive strike. For another, Bush's discourse projects emotioned subjects so invested in the construct of heterosexual marriage that any alteration is made to seem a catastrophic blow to democracy. This point is reinforced throughout the speech. For example, Bush refers to marriage as "the most fundamental institution of civilization"; asserts that its preservation occupies a "level of national importance"; cautions against splintering marriage from its "cultural, religious and natural roots," thereby "weakening the good influence of society"; and aligns the constitutional amendment with "kindness and goodwill and decency" (Bush 2006). Bush's language tries to win assent from Congress and the American people by facilitating a certain kind of emotional attachment to marriage that trades on nationalism and pride in tradition.

Describing this discourse as evidence of little more than "emotion as manipulation" underestimates the rhetorical aspirations of Bush's speech (and of political rhetoric generally). For, what is happening on a larger scale is an attempt to reconstitute the subject by producing emotioned discourse about marriage that will become integrated into the judgments and dispositions of people—that will, in other words, transform people into "objects of feeling" in relation to the marriage construct (Ahmed 2004, 11). However, this example is not merely a case of emotions moving from outside to inside, moving, that is, from the social realm into the personal, individual one. This equation would presume that Bush *has* emotions that he transmits to his listeners, who then take ownership of or disavow them. This explanation presents emotion as something that resides in people, a possession to be shared or withheld. In contrast, the concept of emotion that I want to present in this book looks instead at emotion as emerging relationally, in encounters between people, so that emotion takes form *between* bodies rather than residing *in* them.

This is to say that emotion operates in complex ways—not exclusively an inside-to-outside discourse (self expressing innate feelings outwardly), nor an outside-to-inside one (emotion produced in the social sphere and then internalized by individuals). As Amélie Rorty (1980) suggests in "Explaining Emotions," an inside-outside or outside-inside model of emotion is complicated and ultimately obstructed by histories of emotion, whether individual or cultural, because emotions are a complex blend of at least three factors: first, a "person's psychological past"; second, "the socially and culturally determined range of emotions and their characteristic behavioral and linguistic expressions"; and third, "a person's constitutional inheritance, the set of genetically fixed threshold sensitivities and patterns of response" (Rorty, 1980, 105). Ahmed goes further in her articulation of an alternative to the inside-outside dichotomy by arguing that emotions constitute the border between self and object, making it possible for a person to understand her self/body as an object in distinction to other objects: "[E]motions are not 'in' either the individual or the social, but produce the very surfaces and boundaries that allow the individual and the social to be delineated as if they are objects" (Ahmed 2004, 10). The pertinent question for Ahmed, and for me as well, is not "What are emotions?", but "What do emotions do?" However, whereas her interest is in how emotions "shape the 'surfaces' of individual and collective bodies" (ibid., 1), I am interested in what emotions perform/embody/enact/generate and in how naming emotions affects our relation to the situation in and for which they are named. My study calls attention to the work that emotions do in the context of disciplinary formation, teaching, and administering writing.

It is this focus on emotions as technologies for doing, influenced chiefly by rhetorical and feminist theories, that directs my use of terms in this study. I use *emotion* as the key term, rather than *feeling* or *affect*, because it best evokes the potential to enact and construct, name and defile, become and undo—to perform meanings and to stand as a marker for meanings that get performed. These are rhetorical activities because they have to do with consequences and effects, interpretation and judgment, change and movement. Likewise, experiencing and interpreting emotion entails situational and perceptual components, what psychologist Lisa Feldman Barrett (2005) calls "emotion identification," consisting of "category knowledge about emotion [that] may act like 'emotion stereotypes' to shape our perceptions of emotion in others and in ourselves" (Barrett 2005, 269). By emphasizing categories of emotion as perceived rather than ontologically fixed states, Barrett's work lends support to the idea that emotion is a rhetorical construct requiring a critical vocabulary to enable its rhetoricality to come into full view. *Requirement* is indeed the right word here because of the widely held assumption that emotions are natural biological phenomena. In other words, because people feel emotions and can identify categories of emotion and their familiar manifestations within a particular culture, emotions regularly escape critical thought. I hope to make clear that this oversight leads to a larger omission: neglecting to analyze emotion effects leads to neglecting emotion's role as that which binds the social body together as well as tears it apart, a point of crucial importance to the practice and study of writing and rhetoric.

Returning to terminology, *feeling* is not as useful as *emotion* for me because it suggests the personal, individual experience of emotion and so tends to bring to mind expression or assessment of emotion states (i.e., I feel happy) rather than acts of intention and movement. And *affect* names preverbal, visceral conditions that encompass emotion and feeling. Offering a more precise description of affect, Barrett writes in "Feeling Is Perceiving" that affect involves "[a]ll the neural processes by which an organism judges, represents, and responds to the value of objects in the world" (ibid., 265). Affect refers more to a sense and an atmosphere than it does to a specific, intentioned act of making or unmaking, which I more readily associate with emotion effects. Despite these meaningful distinctions, you may sometimes catch me slipping among these terms simply because they are linked in their capacity to signify emotive functions, and they offer a more textured, because more varied, vocabulary to me.

I also attribute the occasional slippage among terms to a conscious effort to gesture toward the interconnected, dynamic quality of current research. It is striking to me that, as I revise this book in June 2006, sustained critical studies of emotion, affect, and feeling are proliferating at an astonishing rate (see Ahmed 2004; Barrett et al. 2005; Bouson 2005; Brennan 2004; Cvetovich 2003; Marcus et al. 2000; Terada 2001; in composition studies, see Edbauer 2005; Jacobs 2005; Jacobs and Micciche 2003; Levy 2005; Lindquist 2004; Wiederhold 2002; Worsham 1998b; Yoon 2005). Not until the 1990s did we witness sustained interdisciplinary challenges to prevailing ideas that regard emotion as internal, irrational, and natural. Numerous titles in anthropology, architecture, history, philosophy, psychology, the sciences, feminism, and education give some idea of the scope of the widening "affective turn," as it might be called. After the death of the author, the fragmentation of postmodernism, and the rhetoric of reason articulated through the rhetoric of inquiry movement, it seems we are now faced with questions concerning how people, cultures, power, and identity, among other things, may be understood and reconceived through a complex blend of judgment, feeling, logic, and power. But why this interest, and why now?

Having no definitive answer in hand, I would like to speculate about the exigence and timeliness of research on emotion. I see critical study of emotion in the Humanities and Social Sciences as the cumulative effect of postmodernism and rhetorics of difference (including feminism, multiculturalism, cultural studies, and postcolonialism) that have been instrumental in deconstructing the notion of a unified subject. Sooner or later this concentration on the complexity of subjectivity, especially on the social dimensions of experience, identity, and selfhood, would have to produce challenges to emotion's status as natural (because expressed through the body), although it is certainly true that emotion has been the last vestige of the humanist subject, surprisingly free from the critical gaze

otherwise rigorously committed to demythologizing—and politicizing—the essence of virtually every aspect of identity and experience. Without a doubt, the reason/emotion binary has a tight grip
on us, shaping everything from gender stereotypes to beliefs about
the very constitution of knowledge. The process of making unnatural a concept so embedded in our individual and collective socialization is therefore a slow one but, I would argue, a necessary and
inevitable one. Barrett reminds us that "concept undoing" is part of
a larger narrative of progress that, in psychology as in other fields,
has involved fundamental changes in how researchers conceptualize "core" components of selfhood: "Many psychological constructs
that scientists once thought of as fixed, unitary causal entities with
an identifiable essence (e.g., memory, personality, concepts, attitudes) are now thought of as emergent properties or byproducts of
distinct but interacting systems" (Barrett 2005, 277).

Blindness to emotion as a social concept may be attributed to
what feminist theorists have long recognized as the feminization of
emotion, a persistent historical and cultural (at least in the West)
association of emotion with irrationality, manipulation, essence,
and, of course, women—associations that have amounted to emotion's subordinate status in knowledge-building and critical projects
of all sorts (for critiques of this association, see Bartky 1990; Lutz
1990). In conjunction with its feminized status, emotion has been
cast as "soft" and counter-factual, at odds with objective, systematic resources for doing critical analysis. Only feminist scholarship
has consistently capitalized on emotion as a resource for coalition-
building as well as for theorizing experience. In two seminal texts,
Women's Ways of Knowing (Belenky et al. 1986) and *This Bridge Called
My Back* (Moraga and Anzaldúa 1981), feminists mine emotions
and emotion discourses in order to arrive at a better understanding
of women's realities. In effect, these texts, and many others since,
work to de-privatize emotion, making its presence in women's
lives consequential and, in some cases, a problem to be addressed
through political change movements.

But, back to our questions: Why emotion? Why now? It is
because, in part, of postmodern theory and its ironic stance toward
meaning, selfhood, and experience. In the turn to affect, I sense ex-
haustion around postmodernism's emotional cool, its smooth distance from excessive, demonstrative emotion or "soft" sentiments
concerning how people feel, in avoidance of that most uncritical
of indulgences—nostalgia. Produced by meta-narratives that seek
to tie loose ends together, nostalgia is also a product of universal-
izing discourses that project sameness and stability where there
really is difference and uncertainty. However, the ironic distance

of postmodernism has sometimes led to uncritical endorsements of heterogeneity at the expense of embodied realities. Susan Bordo (1990) poses the problem in these terms: "What sort of body is it that is free to change its shape and location at will, that can become anyone and travel everywhere? If the body is a metaphor for our locatedness in space and time and thus for the finitude of human perception and knowledge, then the postmodern body is no body at all" (Bordo 1990, 145). Indeed, related to the affective turn is the growing emphasis on embodiment, performativity, and trauma—all of which represent efforts to become more attentive to the materiality of experience and to better account for emotion effects in relation to group and individual identity formation. And yet, the affective turn has certainly benefited from, perhaps even grown out of, postmodern thinking, especially the broad project of "how to understand and (re)constitute the self, gender, knowledge, social relations, and culture without resorting to linear, teleological, hierarchical, holistic, or binary ways of thinking and being" (Flax 1990, 39). Ann Cvetkovich, in *An Archive of Feelings: Trauma, Sexuality, and Lesbian Public Cultures* (2003), demonstrates both critical attention to *feeling* as a category of analysis and allegiance to a postmodern sensibility that values nontraditional materials and narratives in constructing a political past. She makes a provocative case for understanding trauma as a catalyst for generating cultural archives and political communities. Her interest is in how texts, performances, and activism together constitute an archive of public culture that comes to terms with trauma and forms a site of resistance through which conditions producing trauma become transformed. Cvetkovich taps into the rhetorical function of emotion throughout her study; her emphasis on trauma as part of everyday life, and so not reserved for describing catastrophic events, builds toward the idea that extreme, often painful emotioned experiences can become heightened sites from which to develop strategies of resistance operative within cultures and communities.

In composition studies, reflections on *why emotion, why now* point to the cumulative effect of at least four factors: (1) the absorption of feminist thinking into mainstream composition discourse, resulting in examinations of gendered discourses, concepts of difference, identity and authority problematics, and the politicized dimensions of emotional and intellectual labor, among other foci; (2) the effects of rereading classical rhetoric in pursuit of revisionary histories and renewed understandings of rhetorical concepts (see Quandahl 2003; Walker 2000); (3) the continued influence of interdisciplinary scholarship in composition studies; and (4) the increasing presence of bodies in composition scholarship. While the first three are probably familiar to many readers, I should say a few words about the focus on the body as an area of scholarship that directly connects to emotion research. When I say that bodies have become more present, I mean, in part, to distinguish this presence from earlier efforts to foreground student *texts*, *voices*, and *identities* in scholarly research, which is to say that although earlier works have sought to integrate representations of students as whole persons into scholarly research, rather than construct them as disembodied textual devices, such work has not offered an explanation or theoretical analysis of the body in the text. What is different, then, about the current moment is that focus on the materiality of the body and its performative potential has begun to usher in a theory of writing, as yet unformulated but most certainly "in the air," that explores what embodiment in writing means and why it could or should matter to writing teachers and scholars.

General directions for this promising area of research are already being suggested, particularly within rhetorical theory and queer theory. Working with classical rhetorical theory, Debra Hawhee, in her recent book, *Bodily Arts: Rhetoric and Athletics in Ancient Greece* (2004), explores the body–mind connection among ancient scholars of rhetoric, arguing that performing athletics and doing rhetoric were the conditions of emergence for these scholars and so also for the texts that are identified with the birth of rhetoric and democracy. Her study works at the "interstices between athletics and rhetoric in order to help elaborate rhetoric's emergence in a network of educational and cultural practices articulated through and by the body" (Hawhee 2004, 6). The body is always interconnected with knowledge-making activities, though "the life of the mind" tends to operate as shorthand for doing scholarship, with the body nowhere in sight. Hawhee's study encourages compositionists to ask how explicit acknowledgment of the mind–body continuum may inflect our teaching practices as well as our theoretical and historical projects. Another form of this question is constructed at the intersection of queer theory and composition. In their special issue of *JAC*, guest editors Jonathan Alexander and Michelle Gibson (2004) call attention to queer theory's emphasis on identity as performed and embodied through complex matrices of power, a notion that has implications for how composition teachers prepare students—gay, straight, bi, or otherwise sexually identified—to write and/or analyze narratives of identity (Alexander and Gibson 2004, 7; see also Alexander and Banks 2004). Along with a growing number of scholars, the editors of this special issue ask compositionists to think about sexuality as a discourse intimately connected to how concepts of identity are enacted and transformed in writing (see

Alexander and Gibson [2004] for a useful resource on such work in composition studies and beyond).

Attention to performance and embodiment is also beginning to influence discussions about the value and relevance of academic writing, conventionally measured through the production of traditional essays. This assumption is being challenged, however, by calls for multimodal rhetorics that seek to reconfigure writing as a dynamic process involving a range of materials and strategies, in effect calling into question printed words as the best gauge for judging "writing." For example, a recent study focused on writing pedagogy, "Performing Writing, Performing Literacy" (Fishman et al. 2005), calls for a "flexible critical vocabulary as well as a catalog of the writing and rhetorical situations that call for amplified, performative, and embodied argumentation of different kinds" (ibid., 247). Part of the context for this argument is that students are already immersed in multimedia and other performative discourses on a daily basis; the body is already in the room, thus teachers would do well to construct dynamic writing assignments and, more broadly, to conceive writing in a way that capitalizes on everyday forms of embodiment and performance.

My point in this (extremely abbreviated) discussion is to make the case that body studies and emotion studies emerge from a similar impulse, which I would characterize as a desire to make rhetoric continually accountable to wider sensory and experiential realms and to expand rhetoric's province beyond the effects we have on one another to the larger context of how the resources we use to "effect" get constituted as effectual, come to have particular meanings and associations, and, through this possession, persuade or fall flat. The link between emotion and embodiment has been made explicit elsewhere, notably in interesting new psychological research. In "Embodiment in the Acquisition and Use of Emotion Knowledge," Paula Niedenthal et al. (2005) work at the interstices of emotion and embodiment when they argue that "the acquisition of knowledge about emotion—the perception, recognition, and interpretation of an emotion in the self or other—involves the embodiment of emotional states" (Niendenthal et al. 2005, 22). According to these researchers, we come to know emotion only through its embodied forms, a point that, at minimum, may encourage writing teachers to pause before introducing the Aristotelian pathetic appeal as a kind of plug-in tool for evaluating how a writer "plays on" a reader's emotions. Who is this abstract reader and what embodied realities does she signify to the writer? What counts as an emotional appeal and to whom? I will return to these questions in Chapter Three, where I sketch strategies for "teaching emotion" anew. First, though, because I situate my focus in this book in the interdisciplinary affective turn, my thinking about emotion represents a departure from the more familiar idea that emotion is primarily a tool for persuading an audience to believe something, to form a judgment about something. In the following section, I sketch briefly this default view of emotion as articulated in composition studies in order to give some sense of the departure I'm undertaking.

Emotion in Composition Studies

It is not that I disagree with the idea that emotions move audience thinking, judgment, and behavior. How could I, when these effects are so readily apparent in everyday life? My problem is that as the predominant—and for some writing teachers, exclusive—understanding of emotion in circulation, this view is reductive and disengaged from the complexity of emotion as experience, expression, embodiment, power enactment, and discourse. Another way to say this is that our field has adopted a naïve perspective on emotional experience and perception as constituting acts. Because circulation of emotion meanings in composition studies, until very recently, has been relegated to textbooks and rhetoric anthologies, a brief look at such texts will make clear what I see as common, but insufficient, emotion constructs.

For Patricia Bizzell and Bruce Herzberg, writing in *The Rhetorical Tradition* (2001), "Emotional appeals are something of an embarrassment in the classical system" (Bizzell and Herzberg 2001, 6). They write that ancient rhetors understood that "reason could barely persuade by itself" (ibid.) but also note that the ancients did not address emotion's role in the invention process of formulating a position; instead, emotion is relegated to matters of arrangement or where to put an emotional appeal—and how to put it—to most effectively move an audience.

This view of emotion as a tool we use to appeal to an audience also comprises Edward Corbett and Robert Connors' *Classical Rhetoric for the Modern Student* (1999), in which the authors begin their discussion of the emotional appeal by stating that "[s]ince people are by nature rational animals, they should be able to make decisions about their private and public lives solely by the light of reason. But they are also endowed with the faculty of free will, and often enough their will is swayed more by their passions or emotions than by their reason" (Corbett and Connors 1999, 18). Their explanation of Aristotle's attention to emotion is that, although he wished "rhetoric could deal exclusively with rational appeals,"

Aristotle was a "realist" who understood the sway of emotional responses (ibid.). Corbett and Connors suggest that people need not be "sheepish" about acknowledging the pull of emotions in persuasion, even as the authors complain that "there is something undignified about a rational creature being precipitated into action through the stimulus of aroused passions" (ibid., 77). What's undignified, they explain, is the shame we feel after doing something "under the pressure of strong emotion" (ibid.). Nevertheless, Corbett and Connors assure us that being moved by our emotions is "perfectly normal" and not "necessarily reprehensible," a phrase notable for its inability to develop tolerance of, let alone assign relevance and importance to, emotion's place in persuasion (ibid.).

A more nuanced, invention-based view of emotion derived from the ancients surfaces in Sharon Crowley and Debra Hawhee's *Ancient Rhetorics for Contemporary Students* (1999). In a chapter devoted to the pathetic proof, the authors introduce a number of complicated issues not typically included in rhetoric textbooks. For instance, they point out that emotions are "associated with the body, and are thought to be superficial, dangerous, and feminine" by contemporary rhetors (Crowley and Hawhee 1999, 146). They contrast this negative view of emotion with the more positive and productive uses described by ancient rhetors. Emotions, they explain, were seen by Gorgias as "ways of knowing" associated with "intellectual processes rather than bodily responses" (ibid., 149). Additionally, the authors write that the ancients viewed emotions as a "means of reasoning," as communal and shareable, and as a catalyst for moving people to action (ibid.). Also attesting to some ancient rhetoricians' views of emotion as a way of knowing, in *The History and Theory of Rhetoric: An Introduction* (2001), James Herrick describes a purposeful and motivating use of emotion, remarking that Renaissance rhetoricians were interested in the "emotive power of language," especially in relation to style and elocution (Herrick 2001, 154). Citing views of emotion by Plato, Aristotle, Cicero, and British rhetoricians of the eighteenth century, Herrick even finds that "the relationship between language and human emotion is, thus, a persistent theme in the history of rhetoric" (ibid.).

A persistent theme it may be, but one would not know this by looking at rhetoric-based textbooks designed for undergraduate writing classes. Take, for example, *Style: Ten Lessons in Clarity and Grace* (2003) by Joseph Williams. This book makes no mention of emotion or pathos in its index. Now in its seventh edition and occupying a canonical status among textbooks, this book devoted to crafting a writing style omits emotion entirely. Chapters on elegance and ethics seem appropriate areas where we might expect to find some nod toward a writer's emotional investment in saying something in a particular way, or in developing an ethical stance that emerges from emotioned ways of seeing an issue or problem, but this expectation remains unfulfilled. The absence is especially glaring in a chapter entitled "The Ethics of Prose," in which Williams focuses on the writer–reader contract implicit in any rhetorical situation. The writer's responsibility to be clear constitutes, for him, an ethical imperative to communicate effectively. Underlying this idea is the assumption that writing constitutes a pact through which we commit to social meanings and values. Williams warns that "a writer indifferent to his readers' needs risks more than losing merely their attention. He risks losing what writers since Aristotle have called a reliable *ethos*. Your ethos is the character readers infer from your writing" (J. M. Williams 2003, 187). Generating ethical writing, explains Williams, means that "we would trade places with our intended readers and willingly experience what they do as they read our writing" (ibid.). He further notes that empathy with the reader "puts the burden on us to imagine our readers and their feelings" (ibid., 207). Yet, in his extended stylistic analysis of Abraham Lincoln's Second Inaugural Address, delivered just before the end of the Civil War, Williams limits his discussion of the ethics of prose to sentence-level issues reflecting Lincoln's desire to reconcile the North and South. He identifies, for instance, Lincoln's use of passive constructions, impersonal and abstract language, and nominalized verbs when speaking directly about the institution of slavery.

Williams leaves unsaid numerous opportunities for writing teachers and students to address the relationship among ethics, emotion, and sentence-level decisions. In this particular example, students might consider how the highly emotioned subject of slavery at this point in history led to sentence-level choices through which Lincoln sought to generate unity and displace blame from either the North or the South, especially by referring to God as responsible for the war and its ending. By introducing this sort of analysis, we can encourage students to consider how emotion—in this case, shame, blame, anger, pride, and resentment felt especially by Southerners—is central to the motivation of the speech. More than an "appeal," emotion constitutes grounds for the charged situation during which Lincoln spoke and also shapes his purpose to unite warring factions of the United States. Thus, when Williams notes that Lincoln had reasons to speak abstractly, sometimes misdirecting agency through cumbersome language choices—concluding that doing so was deliberate and ethical—we might ask students to expand notions about clarity and ethics to account for the way these concepts, and the speaking situation, are shrouded in a charged emotional environment that goes beyond a banal desire to tap into an audience's emotions.

More common than the absence of emotion in writing textbooks are warnings of emotion's tendency to deceive and distort. *Everyday Use: Rhetoric at Work in Reading and Writing* (2005) by Hephzibah Roskelly and David Jolliffe presents an example of this bent. They note the use of emotion to create a sense of urgency in an audience, and they point out one of the problematic consequences of the unethical use of emotion that may be incited. Because emotions are "more immediate and sensory," they write, "appeals to the emotions, while dramatic, can also be dangerous" (Roskelly and Jolliffe 2005, 167). This familiar warning about the danger inherent in appealing to an audience's emotions always startles me, for I cannot figure out why a similar warning does not accompany explanations of the logical appeal. Reason and logic are used in our culture (definitely in our government and political system) to incite dramatic responses that may or may not be warranted. They, too, can be used irresponsibly, resulting in dangerous attempts to coerce assent among ill-informed audience members moved by the perceived evenhandedness of reason.

Yet quick judgments about emotion's sneakiness abound, not only in writing and rhetoric textbooks but also in the general presuppositions circulating in composition studies. I came across just such an example in a recent issue of *CCC*. A review by Susan Miller includes the following line, in which Miller summarizes her reading of an author's claims to authority: "In sum, the pathetic appeal is, more than others, unreliable" (S. Miller 2005, 698). Searching the preceding paragraphs to see how she arrives at this claim, I learn that Miller is analyzing Morris Young's authority and use of proofs in his book *Minor Re/Visions* (2004). Finding that his argument depends on emotional appeals, she suggests this is problematic because "in our transitional society . . . consistent empathy with any group, or with ourselves, is almost impossible to elicit from any audience, even ourselves, with any certainty" (ibid., 698). I am struck by this assertion's transparent treatment of emotional appeals as different from others. After all, it must be the case that the success and "certainty" of rational and ethical appeals shift according to situation and audience, too—there is no one instance in which these appeals always get through with *certainty*. Why does Miller, a careful and demanding scholar, find an emotional appeal more suspect, easier to identify as faulty, and more prone to provoke abstract, troublesome concepts such as "consistent empathy" and "certainty"? The embeddedness of emotion in acts of so-called *rational* presentation is mystified by relying on false judgments about reason/logic/facts as credible and trustworthy and emotion as suspect and unreliable. Dismissing the emotional appeals of an argument as somehow more unreliable than others, as Miller suggests, fails to recognize the extent to which all appeals are subject to circumstantial and contextual factors. In addition, as Suzanne Clark (1994) puts it, the "pseudoopposition" between reason and emotion "covers up the vulnerabilities of reason" (Clark 1994, 97). In this way, emotion, and the emotional appeal, are equated with *emoting*, an expression of feeling that speaks from and about the self, and not, as I wish to focus on, emotion as always already present in meaning-making activities. I am not talking about emotion as additive—which assumes that reason, logic, and rationality are normative, staple ingredients—but emotion as integral to communication, persuasion, attachments of all sorts, and to notions of self and other.

To shift our thinking about emotion's rhetoricity requires re-envisioning composition's inheritance from classical rhetoric. Rather than conceiving inheritance as coming into, or taking possession of something by a process of hereditary succession, we need to consider inheritance as an entrustment to build on what came before, a responsibility, in other words, to the present and the future. Inheritance as a measured response to what has come before and an eagerness to look at it through the lens of where we are now. In practical terms, a fuller account of emotion as rhetoric entails not only a rethinking of the classical concepts we have inherited but also a willingness to engage with frameworks beyond classical rhetoric, toward redefinition. This is especially important given that emotion has been cast in a supporting role through extrapolations of classical rhetoric, which largely champion reason, logic, and persuasion as the cornerstones of rhetorical skill. As a result, a tacit assent exists within composition studies through which emotion is made to seem properly located in the margins of rhetoric and writing. This unspoken assumption is only now becoming visible as a steadily growing number of scholars begin to chisel away at emotion's marginality. These emerging critical arguments make clear that emotion matters deeply to the projects of teaching and theorizing writing and rhetoric. As Lynn Worsham (2003) pointed out in her Afterword to my co-edited collection, *A Way to Move: Rhetorics of Emotion and Composition Studies* (Jacobs and Micciche 2003), "[E]motion is the primary object of schooling, wherever schooling happens to occur: in the public sphere, in the family, in the classroom, in popular culture, in high culture, in the workplace, in scholarly texts" (Worsham 2003, 163). With this statement as background, the next chapter examines how compositionists have used emotion as a rhetorical device to generate ways of seeing writing and its instruction, as well as composition's identity as a field.

Note

1. This is not to dismiss the real bodily physical and biological responses to emotion (change in pulse rate, sweaty palms, altered brain activity, and so on). There are links between emotions and physiological responses; however, the identification of bodily changes with certain emotions cannot be divorced from the social world, where naming and interpreting emotions necessarily precedes tracing their physiological functions. In other words, to see how anger affects the body, we need first to agree upon what we mean by *anger*, what its manifestations are, and so forth. This agreement, operating tacitly for the most part, is not biologically objective but arrived at through socialization processes that contribute to the production of feeling subjects. Barrett makes a similar argument, while reviewing existing scientific data, in "Feeling Is Perceiving": "A brief review indicates that after almost a century of searching, scientists still do not have strong, consistent evidence to support the idea that emotions have causal status and produce the substrates for the experience of anger, sadness, fear, and so on" (Barrett 2005, 261).

Chapter Two

Sticky Emotions and
Identity Metaphors

Some forms of stickiness are about holding things together. Some
are about blockages or stopping things moving.
            Sara Ahmed, *The Cultural Politics of Emotion*

Disciplinary narratives and tropes, like personal and cultural ones,
produce affects and feeling subjects. Narratives in general have the
power to attach feeling to scripts of identity and belonging, a lesson I have come to understand more fully through family stories.
Versions of a story that have circulated in my family tell of my
paternal grandfather's habit of buying cars from a local junkyard,
driving them for two or three months until they broke down, and
then going back to the junkyard for one replacement after another.
Growing up, I heard this as a story about poverty, survival, and difference—a young immigrant from Italy trying to make his way in
the U.S.—as well as about humility and the rewards of a "simple
life." I remember feeling proud to hear this story of Richard, née
Diego, told in various configurations over the years (he went to the
junkyard every two weeks, not two months; he sold his cars back to
the junkyard after a bad night of poker and bought them back after
a good one, and so on), because it signaled to me a crafty ability
to get around in the world on a shoestring, to be satisfied with the
small pleasure of a working car, no matter how temporary or bro-
ken down or rusted out it may have been. There is pride in doing

things the hard way because it implies the ability to embrace needs above wants: a life that is not greedy or excessive but is instead frugal and minimalist.

This story narrated to me the value of an emotional world organized around humility and contentment; it also affirmed the idea that residing in the margins is admirable and courageous—worthy of wonder, pleasure, and gratitude. These emotional attachments to the narrative were given more resonance by the embodied image of my grandfather, a long-faced Italian man, always described as gentle and kind (not the usual temperament assigned to Italian men!). He died before I was born, but I have always felt a closeness to him that I attribute to photos as well as to the affective power of narrative—particularly the assimilation (or failed assimilation) narrative. The junkyard narrative, and others that circulate around it, is not just a family story. It is also a positioning tool that, in its retellings, functions as an affective encounter with my own history. It conjures a familial and ethnic identity, which I sometimes embrace and sometimes ignore, based upon the idea that I have benefited from the efforts my grandfather made to construct a life in this country. An insistence made clear through the continual presence and absence of that American symbol of individuality and freedom, the car. There is an identity claim embedded in this narrative, and it circles around the value of persistence, patience, and, above all, modest resourcefulness.

The affect generated and reproduced in this narrative has a "stickiness" about it. The emotions it taps into are ones that "stick" to my identity in ways that I do not fully understand. Emotions of pride, love, and pleasure (associated with the old-time charm of the story—that is, the recollection of days long gone, at least for my family, who own well-running cars these days) both bind me to a certain mythology of history and familial connectedness and block from view the actual conditions of poverty that made the junkyard—if, indeed, the story is accurate—the most apt choice for car-shopping. What "sticks" in this narrative is affect that adheres to family identity.

I borrow the term *stickiness* from Ahmed, who uses it to refer to the "accumulation of affective value" (Ahmed 2004, 92), by which she means that objects—including people, narratives, and a whole host of other signs—amass affective associations that embody and stand for the object. For many people, a Hummer is not simply a vehicle; it accumulates affective valuations that, on the one hand, transform the car into an object of disgust and wildly immoral excess and, on the other, an object synonymous with American-inflected feelings linked to liberty, freedom, affluence, and choice.

In both cases, the object and the affect merge; thus extricating feeling from the Hummer is nearly impossible. Ahmed describes such stickiness as involving "a form of relationality, or a 'withness', in which the elements that are 'with' get bound together" (ibid., 91). This binding is, for her, central to how affect circulates, creating an economy of feeling that gets transmitted and transformed as it moves among bodies and objects. In the discussion that follows, I work with Ahmed's notion of stickiness in order to explore how frequently used identity metaphors in composition discourse involve a sticky "transference of affect" that adheres to notions of the field, composition teachers, and composition courses.

Stickiness is a useful concept for me because it helps explain how emotion resides in neither persons/objects nor the social world exclusively. Rather, emotion is dynamic and relational, taking form through collisions of contact between people as well as between people and the objects, narratives, beliefs, and so forth that we encounter in the world. Ahmed comments on the dynamic quality of stickiness when she says it is "not the property of an object" but rather a substance that "accumulates and affects that which it touches" (ibid.). She continues: "Stickiness then is about what objects do to other objects—it involves a transference of affect [....]" (ibid.). Ahmed's stickiness has to do with circulation, with the economy of affect as it moves between and among bodies and objects. In turn, the circulation of emotion transforms signs into "objects of feeling," a particularly interesting point for my purposes, for it makes available a view of composition teachers and scholars as loaded with feeling that is conveyed through disciplinary and institutional channels—more on that later.

Ahmed identifies repetition as a central rhetorical strategy for creating stickiness among signs, noting that repetition has a "binding effect" (ibid.) as well as a "blockage effect," which "stops the word moving or acquiring new value" (ibid., 92). For her, words or concepts "stick because they become attached *through* particular affects" (ibid., 60). Concentrating on this movement between and among stickiness and affect, in this chapter I explore how metaphors of composition's identity generate emotional subjection that sticks to writing teachers, the composition course, and the field. In addition, I point out some limitations of these metaphors insofar as they participate in what Wendy Brown calls "wound culture," or group identity politics that "becomes [overly] invested in its own subjection" (Brown 1995, 70). My goal is to demonstrate that emotion is not marginal to disciplinary identity, politics, and work; on the contrary, as I stated in Chapter One, emotion binds us together as well as sets us adrift from one another. As we shall see, metaphor is one figure through which we can see emotion working on and through disciplinary identity, its content, and, its discontent.

Composition's Metaphors of Identity

Familiar metaphors in composition studies comment on the field's subordinate status to literary studies, its workers' physical location in basements and shabby, inadequate offices, the prevalence of freeway flyers and gypsy academics, and the placement of first-year writing classes in gatekeeping, service positions. These sites of subordination are meant to correspond to the working conditions of writing *teachers*, but they often come to represent the status of composition as a field of knowledge (in distinction to the composition course) as well as to composition specialists (in distinction to composition teachers). Donna Strickland (2004) describes this slippage as a symptom of the field's managerial unconscious, characterized by a "persistent tendency to align composition primarily with teaching, resulting in an obscuring of the administrative function," a function that involves the management of writing courses (most often) by specialists in the field (Strickland 2004, 47). This faulty alignment, Strickland finds, makes it possible for "composition specialists to speak . . . of the feminization and proletarianization of *composition*, as if the entire field were marginalized because those who teach it—as opposed to those who specialize in it—are economically and ideologically marginalized" (ibid., 49).

I find Strickland's argument persuasive, and I would add to it that the slippage leading to the assignment of marginalized status from the teacher/course to the specialist/field also has to do with the stickiness of emotioned metaphors, the residue that adheres, obscuring the actual basis for the attachments, as a result of pervasive and repetitive claims of low status. In this sense, emotion metaphors are performative, following Judith Butler's delineation of that concept, because they generate effects through processes of reiteration. In addition, the metaphors discussed next fix the field in time, creating a stickiness that blocks new meanings. Ahmed suggests that "fixing" is one function of performativity, which is dependent "upon the sedimentation of the past; it reiterates what has already been said, and its power and authority depend upon how it recalls that which has already been brought into existence" (Ahmed 2004, 92–93). As a result, the identity metaphors that reassert the subordinate status of composition and compositionists "lag behind" the conditions they seek to reveal and critique, unwittingly reproducing those conditions as they do so (see ibid., 93), a point discussed in the final section of this chapter.

The field's marginality is central to its affective standpoint, its members' emotioned way of seeing the work that gets accomplished and obstructed. This standpoint is also a factor of composition's empathetic relation to other subordinate groups. Composition's location functions as a site from which to justify a standpoint that claims to be more egalitarian than other academic fields and more able to see inequitable labor conditions in the academy. This standpoint also generates a special awareness of the potential violence of education programs, effects of which include the dehumanization of students through teaching practices that envision passive learners. The assumption at work here is that because composition has been othered by institutional value systems, it has a uniquely intimate relationship to populations that have been objectified and oppressed in the wider culture. In fact, Chris Gallagher (2005) argues that the streamlining effect of disciplinarity—including the production of insiders and outsiders—causes what he calls "disciplinary guilt" among compositionists who "tend to think of our very mission as legitimizing and rendering audible the discourses of others, *especially* when they are marginalized" (Gallagher 2005, 79).

In addition to signifying writing teachers' poor working conditions, references to composition's marginality are, as I indicated above, references to "The Course," which has generated considerable emotionality among teachers, students, and administrators since its inception (see Connors 1990; Popken 2004).[1] For example, William Riley Parker memorably remarked in 1967 that teaching composition is "slave labor" and that "freshman theme-writing" is a "dismal, unflowering desert" (Parker 1988, 11, 13). He also argues that most Americans assume that composition instruction is essential "despite the fact that it rarely accomplishes any of its announced objectives" (ibid., 11). Parker charges that the location of composition courses within English departments is a marriage of convenience rather than a "true marriage," a point that he predicts will be realized when the federal government subsidizes graduate study, exonerating graduate students from having to teach first-year writing, "a great secret strength for 'English' with both administrators and the public" (ibid., 14). In other words, composition courses are, for administrators, a cash cow and, for the public, incorrectly seen as essential to literacy development. Parker makes clear that teaching writing is a dreadful enterprise involving emotional subjection

---

[1] The remainder of this section, which is focused on composition's marginality, includes sections from a previously published essay, "Emotion, Ethics, and Rhetorical Action" (*JAC* 25.1 (2005): 161–84). In addition, several passages from that essay appear here in slightly revised and expanded form.

for teachers and students as a result of the grueling labor required and the hopeless, "unflowering" nature of the whole enterprise. His characterization highlights something more than a discussion of the intellectual vacancy of teaching composition; he presents the intellectual emptiness as inseparable from the emotional brutality of having to work so hard at something that accrues so little reward. This picture of a composition teacher's emotional labor involves conflicting demands. On the one hand, the teacher is expected to convey optimism about students' progress as writers; on the other, hopelessness, exploitation, and frustration, in Parker's account, are the writing teacher's constant companions.

Literary critic Sharon O'Dair (2000) offers a recent rendition of Parker's dismal view when she refers to teaching composition as a "horrifying situation," a fate that "isn't fun or challenging or respected or rewarded" (O'Dair 2000, 51). She asserts that this is because teaching composition is no longer like it was in the 1950s and 1960s. Today, students often "cannot construct a coherent sentence," creating a situation in which "remediation is almost the norm," rather than refinement of students' considerable writing skills, to which teachers presumably devoted themselves in the past (ibid., 51). With regret, O'Dair also writes that jobs in composition—and minority literatures, which, in her account, fall outside "literature"—have displaced jobs in literature-proper. Despite the decreasing number of jobs in literature, and against practicality and logic, she says that students continue to study it. If these students weren't present in graduate programs, teachers like her might end up having to teach composition, *occasionally*, as she puts it. "Instead of accepting that horrifying situation," she writes, "most of us—professors and graduate students alike—would rather call the situation a 'conundrum' . . .; we would rather up the ante and *take the risk* of grabbing the gold ring, of getting a tenure-track position in teaching literature" (ibid., 50; emphasis in original).

Both Parker and O'Dair construct composition as a site of emotional distress. For O'Dair, choosing composition is not even thinkable as a last resort in desperate employment times. It is clear from the vivid, impassioned language of their descriptions—"dismal," "unflowering," "horrifying"—that composition for them requires self-sacrifice at the expense of a rewarding intellectual life. Their characterizations of the field and the first-year writing course ascribe, from the outside, feelings of hopelessness and dread to both (field and course) through a blurring of the distinctions between them. The negative affect surrounding the teaching of composition, as described by Parker, functions as emotioned residue that sticks, informing O'Dair's blurring of the distinctions between course and

[handwritten margin note: teacher as an emotional emotional distress ally's anxiety]

field. The stickiness of "unhappy" emotions in connection with composition generates a "community of those who are bound together through the shared condemnation" of both the field and the course (Ahmed 2004, 94). Through the repetition of this discourse of condemnation, then, a community is formed as are a set of power relations establishing the norms associated with composition in its multiple configurations—i.e., that it is intellectually deadening, a form of punishment, rightfully approached with dread, thankless and uninspiring, etc. From Parker to O'Dair, we can read a transference of affect from teaching and student writing to the disciplinary configuration of composition.

In contrast, reports from inside the field have sought to understand the forces that make composition a site of ambivalent status and corresponding emotional conflict. That is, within the field are efforts to interrupt and unstick the adhesive that binds composition and dread/despair/boredom by creating a political context around the emotions of intellectual work and, in some cases, establishing an activist agenda to transform writing teachers' working conditions. We see an example of the former, for instance, in Susan Miller's (1991a) explanation of feminization as that which "calls to mind both positive new moves in composition to gender-balance research and teaching and negative associations with the actual 'feminization' of a field that collects, like bugs in a web, women whose persistently marginalized status demands political action" (S. Miller 1991a, 39; see also Enos 1996; Flynn 1995; Holbrook 1991; Reichert 1996; Schell 1992). Miller writes that composition teaching has often been associated with qualities similar to those of the "mythologized mother," including "self-sacrifice, 'dedication,' 'caring,' and enormous capacities for untheorized attention to detail" (S. Miller 1991a, 46). This mother-figure also personifies contrasting qualities such as "authority, precision, and . . . impeccable linguistic taste" (ibid., 46). For Miller, composition teachers are both nurturers and disciplinarians embodying, in either case, strong, distinct emotional dispositions in the classroom. Miller's description of how writing teachers are constructed as feeling professionals reinforces their marginal, feminized status and is a deliberate attempt to draw on the field's emotioned identity in order to establish grounds for politicizing, and so changing, the working conditions of writing teachers.

Other scholars have amplified Miller's critique and call for change, each introducing metaphors that express the emotionality of the situation in slightly different ways. Frances Ruhlen McConnel (1993) chronicles the patch-work employment of "freeway flyers," whereas Eileen Schell (1998b) makes visible the deplorable working conditions of "gypsy academics" and "contingent laborers." Using "women's work" as a metaphor for the subordinate, service-oriented work often associated with teaching composition, Cynthia Tuell (1993) explains that female teachers occupy the roles of daughter, handmaid, whore, and mother. When they are seen at all, Tuell contends, these teachers are seen by administrators and some faculty as "replaceable and interchangeable" caretakers engaged in the "dirty, tedious" work of cleaning up student writing for piecemeal wages and low prestige (Tuell 1993, 126). This list of feminized metaphors describing the working conditions of part-time teachers of writing develops an image of writing teachers as debased, exploited, and dehumanized—an image that has emotional power and consequences. The consequences—not just of these metaphors, but also of the larger argument for improved working conditions of which they are a part—have included labor organizing within composition studies as well as English Studies; professional standards documents on labor conditions issued by WPA, CCCC, and MLA; and a collective awareness of labor conditions as fundamental to the existence and growth of academic institutions.

The larger context shaping composition's emotionally fraught identity and troubling working conditions is its historically marginalized location within English. A great deal of writing has focused on what appear to be "rational" or scholarly explanations of the field's location, although it is safe to say that this writing has been inspired and necessitated by the emotionality entailed in being a neglected field. This writing, in other words, teaches us ways of feeling about location as much as it provides explanations of historical developments that brought us here. One of the primary tools used to accomplish this result has been figurative language—analogies and metaphors that link disciplinary status in the academy with social status in the culture at large. In his contribution to *The Politics of Writing Instruction* (Bullock and Trimbur 1991), for instance, Robert Connors describes the "creation of the composition underclass," identifying composition teachers as members of the "permanent underclass" who are "oppressed, ill-used, and secretly despised" (Connors 1991, 55). In the same collection, James Slevin describes "*all* composition faculty, even those with full-time, tenure-track appointments, as something of an underclass" (Slevin 1991, 7; emphasis in original). Another contributor, Susan Miller, writes that "composition remains largely the distaff partner in a socially important 'masculine' enterprise" (S. Miller 1991a, 40).

Also in this collection, Charles Schuster compares compositionists to Boxer, the equine proletarian hero in George Orwell's *Animal Farm*. Writing specialists, he argues, are the "Puritans of English departments" who "believe both in the ethos of work and, less fortunately, in the beneficence of authority," amounting to a psychology of "professional martyrdom" (Schuster 1991, 87). These faculty, according to Schuster, position themselves as "responsibility bearers" in English departments or "the ones who care about undergraduate education, curricular reform, high school-college articulation" (ibid.). He also describes the work ethic of compositionists as different from others: "Their zeal to teach and serve smothers that other extremely useful instinct: self-survival through the salvation of publishing. . . . Too often they believe that hard work, and hard work alone, will be their salvation" (ibid.). Their dedication rarely pays off, though, as Schuster tells us. Compositionists remain part of the "expendable lower class" consisting of "laborers, factory workers, piece workers" (ibid., 89), a claim that draws an analogy between the work of composition specialists and the exploited labor of the proletariat.

In some cases, the extremity of metaphors of subordination creates an absurd representation of the field's situation. A good example of this is Katherine Gottschalk's (2002) striking overstatement of composition's low status. She compares composition teachers to occupants of an "underdeveloped nation":

> Geographically isolated or marginalized, the composition offices are placed by administrative powers in the poorest accommodations (not infrequently in basements). Members of an underdeveloped nation, staff (often adjuncts—not even citizens) are paid at sub standard rates designed to suit the needs of the colonizing nations who can't afford to treat them better, and who won't locate the classes in their own countries, using their own citizens to teach them. (Gottschalk 2002, 60)

Certainly Gottschalk is correct when she says that writing staff and teachers are treated unfairly and function as expendable members of a department. But when we turn underdeveloped nations into metaphors to describe the conditions of writing instruction, we risk losing sight of the larger context that makes the difference between teaching composition in an American university and living in impoverished conditions very real, not to be glossed for hyperbolic effect. In terms of the power of critique to create change and make us think anew about persistent problems, the strategic value of making arguments about composition's status in these terms is less than effective. Moreover, casting the field as an underdeveloped nation deploys pity as a primary affective disposition, an emotion that is not especially activist in effect.

Gottschalk is not alone in her use of a drastic metaphor to emphasize the extremity of composition's location and labor problem. Nancy Grimm (1999) compares writing center directors to early twentieth-century Irish maids. Like these maids, she says, directors are "very much aware of what sorts of writing and teaching of writing goes on in their university and very intimately involved in that work, yet regularly reminded that they are in service roles, marginalized and excluded from decisions that have direct impact on their work" (Grimm 1999, 14). Grimm writes a compelling narrative account of her female ancestors' arrival in the United States from Ireland. Her grandmother and great-aunts arrived in Pittsburgh where they worked as maids for wealthy families. She notes that research on the working conditions of Irish maids revealed "the round-the-clock beck-and-call schedule and the mandatory wearing of apron and caps that were badges of inferiority" (ibid., 18). Grimm compares her experience as a part-timer earlier in her career to the marked status of these maids: "We part-timers didn't wear aprons to work, but there were other reminders of our status, like not having access to campus parking lots, having our mailboxes in the bottom row, and receiving the letter that came every April bearing the university's logo, the letter reminding us that our contract expired at the end of the term and that there were no guarantees of employment the following year" (ibid.). She also attributes her sense of inferiority as a part-timer and director without a graduate degree to family values passed down through the women in her family whose standard of living was gauged by "how the rich people does it" (ibid., 16). She describes co-editing *The Writing Center Journal* as "[i]mitating the values of the professional 'rich people' in the department" (ibid., 18). Likewise, she earns graduate degrees in order to attain the credentials and status of the "'rich people'" (ibid.). After achieving a permanent position in her department, she writes that her former position seemed not so unlike that of "the Irish maid who is inside but not 'of' the household" (ibid., 20). She suggests that this border identity "may be the position of agency for writing centers in the academy" (ibid., 23). This story ascribes the emotionality of the struggling, hard-working immigrant's story to the experiences of writing center directors. Like the story of Diego with which I began, Grimm's bootstraps narrative, given resonance by the concepts of perseverance and hard work, and given feeling by evoking emotions of hope, longing, and envy, is one that taps into the American ideal of working up from nothing, a heroic narrative that keeps us rooting for the success of the underdog.

The binding between Grimm's maids and writing directors is the experience of alienated labor, which positions both populations as exploited and dehumanized. A similar move is described in

Jennifer Beech and Julie Lindquist's essay, "The Work Before Us" (2004). They claim that "[d]espite our gainful employment, our association with the work of adult literacy does not bring us favored family status; our career path is deemed tantamount to choosing blue-collar over white-collar work" (Beech and Lindquist 2004, 178). Beech and Lindquist also describe English departments as families in which compositionists are the "poor relations" or "those relatives whom the more upwardly mobile of the family would rather keep at a socially safe distance. . . . Our tastes are lowbrow. We hang out with the wrong crowd. We bring too many ill-mannered children to family gatherings" (ibid., 172). Taken together, the metaphors discussed in this section tell us something about the emotional dispositions that accompany compositionists' real and metaphoric work locations in basements, on freeways, in the underclass, in the lower class, and, quite improbably, in an underdeveloped nation. Metaphors of subordination express the frustration, anger, and hurt that result from institutional and intellectual repression and marginalization. It is no accident, then, that pedagogies aimed at empowering students, caring for local communities, especially low-income and indigent communities, and attending to the words and experiences of multicultural writers have been powerful and important agenda items in composition studies. Our emotional investment in serving others and questioning hierarchies that produce them is intimately related to the field's own identity as other within English. Caring for those who regularly slip through the cracks or are viewed as minor, uninteresting, or troublesome—i.e., first-year writing students—is inextricably woven into our mission as a field. Our location in the academy has everything to do with how emotion sticks to the writing, thinking, and teaching we do, as well as to the identity we construct and circulate.

Sharon Crowley (1998) notes that the language of imperialism informs recurring metaphors describing composition teachers as "children, serfs, prisoners, and slaves" (Crowley 1998, 127). Indeed, claiming the field's low status as an identity that expresses something unequivocal and inevitable typifies representations of composition. Links between the oppressed and those of us working in composition reveal a rhetoric of subjection, however, that I believe limits the influence of our collective intellectual work. It does so by nurturing an emotional disposition that relies on feelings of powerlessness and loss. Our low status functions as a connection point, something that we all have in common despite individual status and situational differences. The next section seeks to explain the effects of identity metaphors that mine feelings of dispossession. As I hope to illuminate, these metaphors derive from a will to critique existing institutional and political inequities but ultimately produce a self-subversion of the critique being launched.

Composition's Wound Culture

In composition scholarship, the repetition and ubiquitous aspect of identity metaphors that express emotional subjection have made both critique and installation of marginality a core component of identity. This is not to say that composition research and teaching have not occupied a subordinate position in the academy. To put it mildly, composition teachers and specialists have struggled under the weight of elitist, classed judgments about writing and teaching as less valuable than reading and theorizing. Our histories tell this story strikingly and convincingly; my goal is not to delegitimize that work but to ask what effects the emotional subjection expressed through identity metaphors have on compositionists' political efficacy and intellectual work. The persistence of these metaphors, especially in arguments for institutional change, suggests that they have power to shift thinking and belief, to facilitate a new paradigm for composition. Yet, the conditions remain, as do the metaphors.

In *Metaphors We Live By*, George Lakoff and Mark Johnson (1980) explain that metaphors "form coherent systems in terms of which we conceptualize our experience" (Lakoff and Johnson 1980, 41). Operating as shorthand for a set of experiences, metaphors structure our consciousness by teaching us to see one thing in terms of another. Metaphors also enable (and disable) new ways of perceiving, just as they are always in danger of spiraling into cliché through overuse. When most illuminating and effective, metaphor develops an affective culture around an object, instructing people how to feel about it. For example, the USA Patriot Act of 2001 is the title of a bill passed by Congress and invokes a metaphor that stands for an unconditional allegiance to country. The very name of the bill announces that to be in compliance with it is to be law-abiding, freedom-loving, and concerned about the safety and welfare of every U.S. citizen—to act patriotically. In other words, the "Patriot Act," the short title for "Uniting and Strengthening America by Providing Appropriate Tools Required to Intercept and Obstruct Terrorism," teaches a simple lesson in affective management: care of country is expressed through acceptance of and respect for the bill. Of course, what is blocked in this equation are the details regarding privacy, rights of legal representation, and the many other issues that have emerged as problematic over the past five years. As metaphor, the Patriot Act has altered Americans' perceptions of their vulnerability to terrorism, of the world at large and the dangers it poses to our safety and "way of life."

Lakoff and Johnson point out that metaphors have the power to change perception and thereby experience, leading to a shifting concept of reality:

> This can begin to happen when we start to comprehend our experience in terms of a metaphor, and it becomes a deeper reality when we begin to act in terms of it. If a new metaphor enters the conceptual system that we base our actions on, it will alter that conceptual system and the perceptions and actions that the system gives rise to. Much of cultural change arises from the introduction of new metaphorical concepts and the loss of old ones. (Lakoff and Johnson 1980, 145)

They go on to say that while traditional views see metaphor as only a matter of language, "changes in our conceptual system do change what is real for us and affect how we perceive the world and act upon those perceptions" (ibid., 145–46). I would add that these changes are due not to the workings of metaphor alone, but also to the circulation of feeling through metaphor, an adhesive that binds metaphor to bodies, objects, experiences, and perceptions. Metaphors accrue a certain amount of stickiness through repetition and circulation, shaping constructions and perceptions of reality while creating affective spaces. They participate in a transference of affect that adheres (usually without our notice) through the force of repetition and regularity, as in the case of the American flag—a metaphor that, in the U.S., is meant to evoke pride, strength, and belief in abstract ideals considered crucial to democracy (i.e., justice, freedom, and patriotism). When metaphors harden, replacing descriptive value with a perceived matter-of-fact rendering of how things are, they lose their power to reconstruct, to help us see anew. We are left with the sticky residue that continues to bind affect and object but that does so automatically, without thought or question and, importantly, without the originally desired effectiveness. This process of demetaphorizing metaphor is particularly relevant to composition's identity metaphors, which no longer enact new ways of seeing and thinking but mark and repeat a previous metaphor.

These metaphors develop into what Wendy Brown (1995) calls wounded attachments, or attachments to loss, exclusion, and suffering that become entwined with politicized identity. For Brown, wounded attachments represent a refusal to accept subordinate identities produced through historical processes, as well as a claim for such identities and the acknowledgment of pain and suffering they entail. Although her focus is on political identities as they circulate in U.S. culture, her examination of the paradoxical nature of these identities provides a fresh outlook on the effects of identity metaphors in composition studies. Especially because these metaphors are often presented within the context of developing an emancipatory agenda for the field, Brown's thinking about the tension between the empowering and repressive functions of identifications brings to light composition's fraught discourses around self-presentation and representation.

Brown argues that wounded attachments in minority cultures become identifying marks that subvert efforts toward empowerment. Wounds are evidence of violence and can signify physical places of damage. A wound represents a physical, mental, and political place of hurt and injury; it functions as an authenticating pain that is both a point of contention and a site of shared identity. Brown is interested in how political identity claims are hindered by attachments to pain and marginality, which operate as tropes for what binds people together. To be attached to a wound is to be at once fascinated and abhorred by the vulnerability of the body and the physicality of pain. Such attachment is also a means by which we construct identity and configure difference. Although compositionists have obviously suffered differently than have the minority populations to which Brown refers, wounded attachments also plague compositionists, who are constructed as suffering from emotional subjection and also assert their very marginality as "itself constitutive of the centrality and legitimacy of the center" (Brown 1995, 53). In the context of both politicized identity groups and compositionists, the wound becomes the object of feeling, perhaps even the most compelling site of meaning and identification. In Lauren Berlant's (2000) phrasing, understanding the wound as central to identity involves fetishizing it as "evidence of identity" (Berlant 2000, 34). "As a result," she argues, "minority struggle can get stuck in a groove of self-repetition and habituated resentment, while from the outside it would appear vulnerable to the charge of 'victim politics'" (ibid.). Gallagher describes obsessive focus on a "fear of not mattering" in composition scholarship in terms that sound very much like Berlant's notion of fetishizing the wound: "[T]his fear of not mattering—or, properly, of mattering only to ourselves—is pervasive in composition and rhetoric. And while it is in some respects salutary [...] it also gives rise to what sometimes feels to me (and my students) like an almost neurotic self-questioning" (Gallagher 2005, 76).

This description speaks quite aptly to the situation of composition, perpetually under the thumb of departments, administrators, and institutions that fail to acknowledge the field's value. Composition's identity, to borrow from Brown, "becomes attached to its own exclusion [...] because it is premised on this exclusion for its very existence as identity" (Brown 1995, 73). Such attachments, Brown argues, install "pain over [the group's] unredeemed history in the very foundation of its political claim, in its demand for recognition as identity" (ibid., 74). In her study of political identity formations in late modern democracy, Brown is skeptical about whether identity-based claims can enable the important work of granting political recognition to a group of people without "resubordinat[ing] a subject itself historically subjugated through identity" (ibid., 55). That is, when a group collectively organizes around issues of identity in order to generate conditions for change within that group, how is it possible to use identity as both evidence of a need for change (identity as means of negation) and evidence of identity itself (identity as means of positive identification), without reproducing the subjugated identity in question? Composition studies faces this paradox because its identity has served as the basis for critique as well as the marking of difference in a productive way, particularly in relation to our unique focus on writing, students, and teaching. There is pride in identity but also consistent efforts to disconnect it from "unhappy" emotions and their effects, which include reinforcing the field's subjugation and devalued status within institutional contexts.

Given the amount of scholarship devoted to historicizing, explaining, and revising composition's story, it is appropriate to ask what this investment in identity produces that is usable. And what do these investments make impossible? We might ask, following Brown, "[W]here do the historically and culturally specific elements of politicized identity's investments in itself, and especially in its own history of suffering, come into conflict with the need to give up these investments [...] in the pursuit of an emancipatory democratic project?" (ibid.). Composition's emotional subjection, revealed and reproduced through identity metaphors, is undoubtedly a byproduct of its belief in democratic projects, in more equitable political arrangements. That is, investment in altering the field's status and its workers' conditions is also an investment in democratic configurations. However, the continued use of classed and gendered metaphors reinforces those status problems by making the accompanying affect stick to the field's identity, installing them as metonyms for the primary constellation of emotions that comprise "composition studies."

The wounded attachments that come to authenticate identity in composition are suffused with loss and hurt; the wounds are part of what make us who we are, what give us a sense of shared mission. Composition's emotional and institutional subordination then functions as an identity marker rather than a source of critique and change. If we are not handmaiden to English, the neglected stepchild, the marginalized other, then who are we? The habituated self-presentation as subordinate offers no real place from which to move the field forward; rather, it amplifies what we already know while failing to map out new meanings through which composition might come to construct alternative, forward-looking identifications. Also, feelings of dispossession and hurt get bound together with those who teach writing courses and with the field itself, enabling the continued blurring of teacher/course with specialist/ field. These categories become interlaced through an overarching emotional disposition that gets expressed through metaphor (and surely other discursive means).

Because metaphors shape the ways in which we see ourselves and conceive the work of the field, we should consider how to construct metaphors for composition in renewed language that resists positioning ourselves as principals of our own subjection. This will entail critical work on emotion as a fundamental component in the making of knowledge, the formation of disciplinary identity, and the development of teacher efficacy. We need multiple vocabularies and explanatory frameworks, in other words, to unstick "bad" affect from composition.

Understanding emotion as an analytical tool that helps us to see how composition has gotten bound up with dread and frustration implies rejection of "the steady slide of political into therapeutic discourse" (Brown 1995, 75). This is worthy of comment because, for many of us, the first association upon mention of "emotion" often involves assumptions about individually experienced feelings or expressions through first-person narrative. A telling example appears in *What to Expect When You're Expected to Teach* (Bramblett and Knoblauch 2002), edited by graduate students at the University of New Hampshire. With a title playing on the *What to Expect* series of books for first-time parents, this book compares first-time teaching with the sometimes terrifying act of first-time parenting. Billing itself as a "site for honesty" (Bramblett and Knoblauch 2002, x) in which contributors break "the silence of failure and anxiety" around teaching (ibid., xi), this collection aspires to be read as a sourcebook, referenced in times of crisis, rather than a linear, scholarly argument. *What to Expect* took form, the editors tell us, because teachers, especially novice ones, "needed to hear that everybody screws up, and that screwing up doesn't make you a bad teacher. It's absolutely, totally, and completely NORMAL" (ibid.). This book validates the emotional component of teaching, by which the editors mean feelings of bewilderment, anxiety, and anger (ibid., xiii). In his introduction, Thomas Newkirk tells us that the book offers an important antidote to the "consistently upbeat success stories" that fail to "capture the emotional underlife of teaching" (Newkirk

2002, 3). In most accounts of teaching, Newkirk says, "the teacher never shows signs of despondency, frustration, anger, impatience, or disappointment" (ibid.). Newkirk urges teachers to be "honest" in telling their stories and to no longer hold close their secret failures and misgivings (ibid., 8).

The emotionality surrounding teaching, as represented in this collection, is closeted because revealing anything less than success in the classroom is asserted to be nearly unspeakable in composition scholarship. However, a number of texts and articles produced over the last decade detail the "dark side" of teaching, to use Newkirk's phrase, although not always in first-person narratives. For instance, *Outbursts in Academe* by Kathleen Dixon (1998), *Collision Course* by Russel Durst (1999), *Lives on the Boundary* by Mike Rose (1989), *Blundering for a Change* edited by John Tassoni and William Thelin (2000), *Bootstraps* by Victor Villanueva (1993), and articles by Wendy Hesford (1998), Shirley Wilson Logan (1998), Richard Miller (1994), Piper Murray (2003), and Lad Tobin (1991), among others, address what happens when teaching fails, exhausts and frustrates teachers (and students), uncovers offensive prejudicial thinking among students, and gets mired in mediocrity and tedium. The "secrets" of the trade are spoken in these and other accounts, although not in the confessional mode. *What to Expect* teaches that being "honest" and unveiling "secrets" about teaching, usually having to do with failure, require personal writing and emotioned confession about individually experienced anxiety pangs. The value of emoting in this text, understood as revealing something about the writer's private feelings and about the truth of how "we all" feel, is mirrored in how most of us teach the emotional appeal in our classrooms. Rather than looking at how the grounds of our work—what binds us to teaching, writing, and, often, championing literacy education—is emotioned in a broad sense, we tend to focus on expressions of feeling about personal experience as evidence of emotioned writing. As a result, what counts as *emotional* to us and to our students remains in the feminized realm, cordoned off from the work of reason and intellect and reserved for journaling and other forms of private writing. Although *What to Expect* offers valuable insider information to newcomers in the field, what bothers me is that its investment in a privatized, experiential construct of emotion reflects a larger tendency in composition to undervalue emotion as a rhetorical, performative enactment. In other words, these associations with emotion predominate in composition scholarship, short-circuiting more complicated understandings of how emotion creates an economy of feeling that constitutes and transforms who we are and what we do.

Wendy Brown's suggestion at the end of "Wounded Attachments" poses a provocative challenge for composition, one that necessarily

[handwritten marginalia: makes me concerned b/c EdTPA suppressed emotional component of teacher]

demands a reformed concept of emotion, away from the personal experience model just described. She calls for a shift in discourse from ontological definitions to the language of political desire: from "we are" to "we want." Brown asks, "How might democratic discourse itself be invigorated by such a shift from ontological claims to these kinds of more expressly political ones, claims that [...] inhabited a necessarily agonistic theater of discursively forging an alternative future?" (Brown 1995, 76). For her, the sovereignty of the subject in political discourse burdens political effectiveness by always centering claims for change in the "I" rather than the more collectively realized "we." Brown makes the point this way:

> What if "wanting to be" or "wanting to have" were taken up as modes of political speech that could destabilize the formulation of identity as fixed position, as entrenchment by history, and as having necessary moral entailments, even as they affirm "position" and "history" as that which makes the speaking subject intelligible and locatable, as that which contributes to a hermeneutics for adjudicating desires? (ibid., 75)

Brown's idea emerges from an assumption that linguistic performatives have potential to enact change. Additionally, however, she's posing an entirely revised framework for articulating identity claims, with the underlying goal of shifting how we think about the political effectivity of identity. One way to begin this work might be to construct new metaphors for composition's identity that emerge from our intellectual work rather than from our wounded attachments to the still extant structures of subordination. Because identity metaphors are tools for explaining who we are to ourselves, mining different caverns of experience and expertise might produce new insights about our potential, creating sites of hope and meaning through which to conjure a different sort of affective stickiness.

Of note, while Brown wants a language that no longer fetishizes wounded attachments, her proposal acknowledges that wounds and pain are real. Thus, transcending the wound is not the point, nor is detaching from a history of inequality (see Ahmed 2004, 172, for a critique of these ideas in Brown). The point is to use the energy and feeling surrounding wounded attachments as generative grounds for change, a strategy that tacitly shifts us toward performativity as a framework of exciting promise.

Performative Composition

Configuring disciplinary identity as generative and in-process is premised on the idea that disciplines are not fixed locales but creative forms shaped by changing forces and conditions and continually reformed by critical, imaginative interventions. With this emphasis on change, I do not mean to proffer an ecology metaphor as that which can provide us with a new way of projecting the field forward. Rather, I have in mind something akin to Donna Haraway's cyborgian myth (1990): creative, playful, politically serious, without origins. Her cyborg figure is constructed as part of a utopian socialist feminist project to imagine "a world without gender, which is perhaps a world without genesis, but maybe also a world without end. The cyborg incarnation is outside salvation history" (Haraway 1990, 192). Constructing the cyborg this way, Haraway reminds us that returning to origins, hoping for redemption and transcendence, always triggers a search for wholeness that eludes, antagonizes, and frustrates, for wholeness rests upon an impossible notion of organic community. What she proposes instead is an ironic manifesto that is "about contradictions that do not resolve into larger wholes" (ibid., 190). Irony, she writes, is "also a rhetorical strategy and a political method" (ibid.).

Reading Haraway's alternative mythology of a world without origin stories—and so without innocence—presents a useful (and playful) heuristic from which to imagine composition's mythology, or counter-mythology, as relayed through metaphors of subordination and as-yet-unrealized possibilities for making and remaking identity. Her ambitious project suggests to me the need for rhetorical strategies to shift our center of gravity from a persistent preoccupation with identity to something less centered, less needy, and tiredly self-referential. One possibility is to consciously resist identity stories in their familiar sense, often grounded in negative metaphor, in order to make use of the performative effects of "composition studies" as name for place, practice, theory, activism, literacy, and more. *Performative* here includes and goes beyond theatrical practice to encompass "action that incessantly insinuates, interrupts, interrogates, antagonizes, and decenters powerful master discourses" (Conquergood 1995 via Bhabha 138). In other words, as D. Soyini Madison and Judith Hamera (2006) argue, "Just as performativity is an internalized repetition of hegemonic 'stylized acts' inherited by the status quo [a view introduced by Judith Butler], it can also be an internalized repetition of subversive 'stylized acts' inherited by contested identities" (Madison and Hamera 2006, xviii–xix). Performativity is about performing or enacting identity in order to contest and dislodge fateful origin stories that slow forward motion.

I am talking, then, not about a substitution of one metaphor for another, but about a changed source/site/referent for the construction of metaphor—a whole different starting place, for as Lakoff and

Johnson put it, "[n]ew metaphors have the power to create a new reality" (Lakoff and Johnson 1980, 145). New metaphors emerge from comprehending our experiences outside the accustomed ways, an altered framework that becomes the basis for *acting* "in terms of" a new reality (ibid.). Thus, refusing composition, the stable, known, static identity—which entails resisting the familiar plot-lines that have come to constitute identification—in favor of performative composition embraces an identity that is "provisional, in-process, existing and changing over time, in rehearsal [...]" (Schechner 1998, 361). This is another way of saying that professionalization is not the end of the story for composition, nor is it the path to redemption, equity, and/or legitimacy. If composition is still in-process, not stabilized by its many markers of professionalization (i.e., book series, graduate programs, journals, conferences, and distinguished scholars), then perhaps this in-between status can be projected as a site of possibility rather than professional marginality.

For example, there is a shift when we think about composition's "space" rather than its "location." In composition discourse, location does not have to, but most often does, mean subordination. However, space is transforming before our eyes as sites for teaching expand to include online technologies and service-learning initiatives, and as research possibilities continue to be transformed by online databases that extend access in exciting new directions. In terms of composition's articulation, location is closed, a trap, an already defined limit; space can designate new territory, a series of openings, a limitless vista. Studying the space of composition, the field and the course, provides a widened view for materialist analysis, one that is better equipped to deal with rapidly changing sites that are less often fixed or knowable, and more often makeshift or random. Foregrounding space, we are able to talk about the many ways in which the field has become recently dis/re/located. Composition programs are increasingly being located outside their traditional home department of English, functioning as freestanding fields of study with distinctive curricula, hiring practices, and degree programs. In these situations, the field is not as easily positioned as the poor, lowbrow relative or as an underdeveloped nation. Instead, it is defined by new relationships, by different experiences and perceptions of identity. Because composition's place is not fixed or predetermined, spatial metaphors seem more capable than those of location to open the field's identification and to resist rendering it as already known.

Changing the metaphor affects the narrative of composition: what the field is defined by and against, and how its story takes form. Changing the story from one about marginality to one about centeredness also alters the emotional content of composition, perhaps offering a break from the rhetoric of subjection. It will be interesting to see how we might use emotion discourse toward positive effect, toward the construction of subjects for composition who challenge the emotional lack generally associated with composition studies, its workers, and its students. Metaphors of subordination, which tend to produce a culture of paranoia and defeatism, generate feelings of inadequacy that too easily become the central subject position from which claims are made.

Instead of enumerating the ways in which "composition is low," then, we might ask, "What does composition enable and enact as practice and theory?" Further transitioning from statement of fact to options for inquiry, let's move from "writing is debased and so are its teachers" to "how can writing be seized to construct counter-truths and playful myths that upset naturalized identities (without minimizing or neglecting the systemic realities of labor inequities)?" The point is that questioning metaphors and their effects leads to asking new questions and eventually to performing identity differently. It also originates political claims from somewhere besides essentialized identity and its accompanying emotional subjection. As Haraway writes, "Innocence, and the corollary insistence on victimhood as the only grounds for insight, has done enough damage" (Haraway 1990, 199).

In making this argument, I have sought to model one possible way to use emotion as a category of analysis. The following chapter extends this effort and builds on my sense that performativity constitutes a productive theory of enactment by which we can materialize emotion and invent pedagogical strategies committed to foregrounding emotion as embodied and lived. In addition, performative pedagogies put a premium on movement and play in the classroom, which are vital for cultivating wonder, an affective disposition that I see as the heart of critical writing, thinking, and teaching.

Chapter Three

Emotion Performed and Embodied in the Writing Classroom

[E]xperiencing an emotion, like conceptualizing in general, may be a skill.

Lisa Feldman Barrett, "Feeling Is Perceiving"

The idea that *experiencing* an emotion—not expressing, perceiving, or analyzing one—may require *skill* represents a titanic shift in thinking about emotions, as does Barrett's (2005) link between experiencing an emotion and the act of conceptualizing. The latter introduces a simple but important point: emotion is central to what makes something thinkable, which is to say that the act of conceptualizing inserts emotion into thought and so into experience, the social world, politics, the whole shebang. In the previous chapter, I sought to position emotion as a category of analysis, illustrating that composition's identity metaphors exceed description of a status location. They indicate an affective disposition that sticks to the field and those associated with it, creating paradoxical opportunities for disciplinary change in the process. In this chapter I turn my attention to writing pedagogy in an effort to conceptualize emotion as thinkable within the classroom. I do so with the effect of Barrett's sentence fresh in my head, helping me to remember the importance of wonder in sustaining and replenishing scholarship and teaching.

In thinking about the value of wonder to teaching and writing, Ahmed is again helpful to me, as she introduces what she calls *feminist wonder*, a version of *critical wonder*, both of which are "about recognizing that nothing in the world can be taken for granted, which includes the very political movements to which we are attached" (Ahmed 2004, 182; for more on critical wonder, see Covino 1988). Ahmed describes wonder as embodied and linked to one's sense of positionality in the world: "[T]he very orientation of wonder, with its open faces and open bodies, involves a reorientation of one's relation to the world. Wonder keeps bodies and spaces open to the surprise of others" (Ahmed 2004, 183). Like emotion, wonder is extralinguistic and so regularly falls beyond the peripheral vision of our primarily text-based focus in composition. Yet, there are good reasons to pay attention to what is around the written because this less defined space is where meanings and attitudes take form, adhere, and become part of the swirl and stick of affect (see Conquergood 2002; Edbauer 2005). Wonder certainly tends to circulate without much critical attention or recognition, despite the fact that we *need* it in order to invest ourselves in the world, in our work, family, education, and so forth. Within the context of composition studies, wonder is a crucial ingredient for "critical thinking" because it is bound up with surprise, curiosity, withholding judgment, and openness to possibility. Wonder, like emotional experiences generally, is not something we simply *have*; having it, or experiencing it, involves what Ahmed calls *capacity* and Barrett calls *skill*. Thus, wonder and other emotional experiences may be considered teachable both outside and inside the classroom—a strange and perhaps counterintuitive idea, one that may even seem beside the point in the context of teaching writing. After all, why should writing classrooms be sanctioned as spaces where emotions are "taught," and what does it even mean to *teach* emotion?

These questions give some indication of the difficulty entailed in making the rhetorical dimensions of emotion "teachable" in the sense of *what to do in the classroom*. Interdisciplinary research on teaching and emotion bears out this difficulty as it focuses primarily on emotion's role in the context of teacher identity, efficacy, and work practices and conditions[1], with scant attention given to how one may actually teach students to deploy emotion as a critical term that yields valuable insights otherwise obscured. Yet the absence of attention on teaching a complex rhetorical view of emotion is in many ways understandable given that emotion has been for so long a naturalized concept, considered irrelevant to serious critical work, outside knowledge, and detached from legitimate forms of argumentation. To present emotion as a teachable critical term involves a wholesale rethinking of what is "teachable" as well as what counts as necessary and usable knowledge in the context of writing and rhetoric. In addition, as rethinkings of emotion continue to proliferate, simplifying rhetorics of emotion by transforming theoretical ideas into classroom lessons threatens to dilute the potential power of adventurous thinking. D. Diane Davis (2000) writes about this threat in her irreverent book, *Breaking Up [at] Totality*, in which she describes the struggle enacted by rhetoricians to "extract themselves from comp's lethal grip" (Davis 2000, 7). Davis argues that studying rhetoric only for the sake of teaching composition leads to rhetoric "getting the squeeze" and losing its rhetoricity (ibid.; see also Worsham 1991). I am conflicted on this point. On one hand, I am troubled by the reductive, conservative effects of mainstreaming knowledge for the sake of making ideas teachable. On the other, I recognize that teachers are excited by new developments in the field and want guidance toward thoughtful, effectual implementation.

With cautious optimism, then, this chapter offers a revised theoretical framework and a set of practical strategies for teaching emotion as a critical and generative category of analysis. Inserting emotion into thought, into the field of meanings where rhetoric operates, gives students a chance to understand and seize upon writing's rhetoricity anew, grasping its potential to shift, nudge, hurt, and heal. More specifically, I focus on the productive, creative, and meaningful effects of teaching emotion as performative and embodied. Much of what I say is speculative and propositional in that I do not narrate already worked-through ways of teaching emotion. Rather, I present several approaches for envisioning, describing, and employing emotion as a critical term with and for our students. My perspective is backwards in orientation, as the approaches I sketch here take form while looking back on classroom moments that could have gone differently. I mostly hope to cultivate a sense of wonder—openness, curiosity, and suspension of disbelief—in relation to how we do language and how our students may also once we admit emotion legitimately and rigorously into the mix.

Emotion and Performativity

The body believes what it plays at: it weeps if it mimes grief. It does not represent what it performs, it does not memorize the past, it enacts the past, brings it back to life. What is "learned by body" is not what one has, like knowledge that can be brandished, but something one is.

Pierre Bourdieu, *The Logic of Practice*

If emotion is not *in* a text, body or culture, as I suggested in the previous chapter, but is produced during collisions of contact, then how do we make collisions the site of instruction? How do we teach something that happens *in relation*, an idea that departs significantly from the identification of emotion as an appeal that can be isolated and identified? How do we ask students to grapple with, and perhaps employ, the extralinguistic quality of emotion? In what can we ground the study of descriptors such as aura, sense, gesture, or atmosphere? These sorts of questions, which suggest that emotion does not reside *in* things and people, indicate that an exclusively text-based approach to teaching reading and writing is ill-equipped to account for the circulation of affect and its ability to stick, to generate interpretations not available through traditional analysis.

An alternative framework for examining how meanings take form and circulate, *performativity* offers promising potential for critical study of the claim that "subjects *do* their emotions; emotions do not just happen to them" (Zembylas 2003, 115). As a practice, an epistemology, and a concept—performativity is the heart of the field of performance studies, a cross-disciplinary venture whose identity is not fixed or clearly demarcated.[2] Richard Schechner describes the field's fluidity as "*fundamentally* relational, dynamic, and processual" (Schechner 2002, x). Although performance studies configures itself as "in process," there is discernible common interest among the field's diverse group of scholars, teachers, and artists in how cultures and identities take shape through rituals, customs, and behaviors. As Nathan Stucky and Cynthia Wimmer (2002a) explain, "Performance studies examines the continually expanding range of behaviors invented by human beings to communicate with each other, especially those which are rehearsed, replayed, or consciously constructed" (Stucky and Wimmer 2002a, 11). Fittingly, then, examining texts, objects, visual forms, movements, and such through the lens of performance studies involves regarding each as "practices, events, and behaviors, not as 'objects' or 'things'" (ibid., x). Hence, performance studies includes and goes beyond the "theatrical" to encompass "how human beings fundamentally make culture, affect power, and reinvent their ways of being in the world" (Madison and Hamera 2006a, xii). This view of human action corresponds to the idea that emotions are enacted, not just sitting there to be tapped by a writer/speaker or reader/listener. They are interactive; emotions take form, and then take on other forms, or become fetishized as fixed forms between people.

This "betweenness" is a function of emotion's performativity, its ability to reiterate norms (following Judith Butler) and to subvert them through "'stylized acts' inherited by contested identities"

(Madison and Hamera 2006a, xix). To talk about the performativity of emotion, then, is to signal both emotion's conservative capacity to produce and reiterate feelings that fix the status quo (patriotic bumper stickers, sports team sweatshirts, and magnetic car ribbons do this) and its disruptive capacity to generate feelings that challenge the status quo (Jesse Jackson's speeches, political rallies, and guerilla theater tend to have this effect). As these examples may suggest, performative acts are "layered in the day-to-day, yet they are heightened and embossed in cultural performances" (ibid.). Everyday performances of any sort—those constructing, for instance, identity, experience, or family history—are constituting acts in that they help to articulate who we are and how we live through crafted narratives and familiar plot-lines. They are also transformative acts capable of crafting new, shifting narratives that help us to live differently. What is clear, returning to Barrett's epigraph at the beginning of this chapter, is that, whatever their effects, emotion performatives require *skill* to enact, because they are responsive to context, and demand an ability to interpret and perform emotioned meanings considered "appropriate" or "inappropriate" in a given context. Although Barrett does not use the term *performative*, her remarks reinforce this idea in a different register, as she emphasizes the centrality of *simulation* to emotional experiences and expressions: "Presumably, there is no single experience of *anger*, but many, dependent on the content of the simulation. It is a skill to simulate the most appropriate or effective representation, or even to know when to inhibit a simulated conceptualization that has been incidentally primed" (Barrett 2005, 274–75). Simulation, and its association with appearance, imitation, and resemblance, not to mention deception and pretending, is linked to the performative insofar as both are extralinguistic expressions involving the body, scripts of one sort or another, play, and liveness.

When we conceive emotion in terms of performativity, we abandon obedience to strict textual analysis that leads quite often to formulaic studies of Aristotle's appeals, which are frequently treated as static, isolated claims that can be identified in a text, or more precisely, in a sentence or paragraph. In assuming emotions are accessible exclusively through language, we fail to grapple with their performative and embodied aspects. The extralinguistic quality of emotion leads to messier, harder-to-clutch meanings that circulate around and through texts, people, classrooms, and cultures—a set of meanings best accessed through a conjoined emphasis on performativity and embodiment, because the body is the site through which emotions are imbued with liveness. "Performance involves the embodiment of language and emotion and the fashioning and display of the body and its affects," writes Michalinos Zembylas in his description of the triangulated relationship among performance, emotion, and embodiment (Zembylas 2003, 119). This is another way of saying that emotions are mediated by the body; they are made visible on and through the body via posture, facial expression, voice, and movement, just as they are perceived in others through these and other embodied signs. Ahmed points out that conceiving emotion as mediated "reminds us that knowledge cannot be separated from the bodily world of feeling and sensation; knowledge is bound up with what makes us sweat, shudder, tremble, all those feelings that are crucially felt on the bodily surface, the skin surface where we touch and are touched by the world" (Ahmed 2004, 171).

When we transfer Ahmed's idea from the general category of knowledge to the specific act of writing—a technology of knowledge—we get closer to understanding how bodies and emotions are not only enacted in writing but also imbued in how we come to writing. Mady Schutzman (2002) makes this point succinctly: "Our physicality affects how we think and how we write, and the page is a stage upon which those physical meanings are put into motion" (Schutzman 2002, 287). What she describes as an enactment of physical meanings through writing became apparent to me, quite accidentally and only in hindsight, after teaching an advanced composition course in winter 2006. My class was not centered on body and emotion issues in relation to writing, but organized around the subject of everyday metaphors. Using Dona Hickey's textbook, *Figures of Thought* (1999), I asked students to write steadily, read frequently, and think creatively and critically about how metaphor structures our thinking, behavior, communication, and cultural narratives and desires. Students were expected to apply concepts made available in the readings to subjects of their own choosing. The first unit of readings dealt with the writing process, writerly identity, and writing about place. Subsequent to our discussion of these themes, students created blog entries about their writing processes, in which I asked them to develop metaphors depicting how they experience writing.

Looking back, I'm surprised that I did not notice at the time that my students' metaphors for writing were nearly exclusively bodily-based. The students' strong connections between embodied experience and writing are instructive to me and certainly go beyond parroting class discussion. After reading Anne Lamott's "Shitty First Drafts" (1999), students posted blog entries in which they crafted metaphors for their writing practices that used as their source material constipation, having a heart attack, and athletic practice, as well as descriptions of bodily activities associated with getting started: walking, smoking, drinking coffee, and drinking beer. Students wrote about how bodies and writing are entangled in everyday, constant ways, as the following excerpts illustrate:

> I like to think of my first draft as a heart attack. The pain of sitting in front of my computer and not having a clear concept in my mind is like the blockage in an artery. It just keeps building until I can't stand it any more. I associate the tingling in my left arm with my stiff body from sitting in the same position for so long. Finally the panic that something is wrong and the fact that I need help sets in. Usually a beer is had in the place of Bayer aspirin to save my life. After I have relaxed I can definitely get some words down and the flow of just writing is my physical therapy into the next draft. Once my ideas are down on paper I have a much more clear view of what direction to take with my writing. The purpose of the paper has clarity and I am out of the danger zone (Spiker).

> As so profoundly described in class, [the first-draft] stage could also be called the "vomit stage." Although, I just pour out all of my first thoughts onto the page I also have a waiting process where I just wait until the ideas become abundantly flowing from my fingertips—however, ironically as long as I wait sometimes the ideas do not seem to come; therefore making me resort back to that "vomit-like" process I detest. Once the relief takes over that I finally have something in paper form, I quit (Sargent).

> Thus it begins again. The cold sweats, the over-caffinated shaking hands, and the act of setting "page goals" for cigarette breaks—these are the days of my essay writing life. It never gets any easier. One would think that after a decade of writing papers that something would change but it doesn't, I am still that fourteen year old girl sitting at my old IBM wondering if I should just play another round of "Oregon Trail" or type another sentence. I guess the only difference is now I shop on EBay instead of playing the game, I buy shoes instead of corn—what a deal.[....] Needless to say, as I pause in my rant, I really enjoyed Lamott's essay. I write crappy first drafts and unfortunately, unlike the verbal vomit that some people speak of, my experience is more comparable to constipation. I push, and prod, and eventually I produce something and get some relief. This something is by far not the finished product, but it is a beginning and the process has been set in motion (Hughes).

> Writing is like taking my dogs for a walk, first I get everything started by announcing "puppa getta go", then I get the necessary tools together, leashes, shitty bags, coat, gloves, flashlight, cell phone, keys, and of course my own wardrobe [....]. Walking is a ritual that I perform three to four times a day, I can't avoid it because the dogs must go, and there are certain things that I must do to prepare for it. Writing is the same way, I write regularly for school whether I want to or not, I have to prepare for distrac-

tions, and eventually I have to decide which way I want to go. Like dogs, every writing assignment is different, some require steady attention to details, and others are more unpredictable. Once I get going with walking or writing it is a simple matter of keeping everything on track, and stopping every now and then to throw away the shit.

The energy, feeling, and humor in these excerpts call attention to writing as a material practice that inevitably gets mixed up with bodily activities and experiences. My students remind me that they *already* know quite a lot about emotions as mediated by the body during the act of writing and about performative enactments—extralinguistic activities evoking certain scripts for writing, habits developed in relation to getting words, and patterns evolved to get through stuck periods. That students already know these things in a somewhat intuitive way seems to me an excellent basis from which teachers might reengineer thinking about emotion, leading to a reinvigoration of practice—perhaps allowing some play into the classroom by doing so—and to a way of opening language, feeling, and persuasion to students. The sort of opening I mean to evoke is one that invites wonder. Rethinking emotion at the convergence of performativity and embodiment engages imagination and inquiry, and offers a means for intervening in closed views of writing and rhetoric that have predetermined the place of emotion before grappling with it in any sustained fashion.[3] The remainder of this chapter describes several pedagogical approaches aimed at putting emotion into serious classroom play.

Deep Embodiment

I describe here a strategy that asks students to focus on embodied emotions. My ideas evolve from examples offered by performance studies scholar Nathan Stucky (2002), who has developed a set of activities aimed at getting acting students to experience what he calls *deep embodiment* (culled from Geertz's concepts, *thick description* and *deep play*). He builds his approach on everyday life performance (ELP), which requires students to "tape-record naturally occurring interaction, transcribe it carefully in the manner of conversation analysts, and then learn to perform it by carefully replicating the intricate detail, the paralinguistic and interpersonal complexity, of the original" (Stucky 2002, 132). The idea is to immerse students in the dynamic intricacies of human interaction so that each student "virtually shares the breath of another person" (ibid., 131). The assignment is designed to generate empathy for the embodied life experiences of others, to come into contact with difference through the study of language that evolves into a practiced way of seeing another's distinct embodiment in the world. One 34-year-old male student reports, for instance, that while performing a 13-year-old girl's language and comportment during class, he recognized that both he and the girl "engage our bodies to communicate the clustering of emotions that are bundled in our everyday performance" (ibid., 135). The student comes to know the girl, of course in a limited and incomplete but nevertheless more nuanced and attentive way, through the use of his body while imitating her talk (ibid., 136). Stucky explains that one of the outcomes of this assignment is to position performance as an "investigatory tool" through which the "act of performance is the study of the interactional moment of an other body, an other human experience" (ibid.). The value of doing so, he suggests, evolves from how "the body can learn from interrogating other bodies through enactment" (ibid., 138). Finally, deep embodiment using ELP resists exoticizing, parodying, or possessing others, according to Stucky, because the "actor's body must accommodate the other, not conquer it" (ibid.).

What I like about Stucky's approach is that it gets students moving, both mentally and physically, and requires them to think critically about embodiment as a process that affects a whole set of relations to world and other. To understand emotion as embodied is to know that it is not static or fixed or predictably available for analysis. I adapt Stucky's exercise for an assignment in which the act of performance functions as an occasion for probing the stickiness of emotion—how emotion resides not in things or people but is produced between them. Emotion takes up residence in people and places such that the operations producing it become invisible, forgotten, overruled by the person or object characterized by or associated with a particular emotion (sometimes to the point of essentialism). In contrast, I would like students to forget the signifier of emotion for a moment in order to remember, or comprehend for the first time, the process that led to the adherence of emotion *to* a signifier. My hope is that students will scrutinize emotion as a rhetorical concept that appears on the surface of things only as a result of complex processes that operate out of sight.

The performative aspect of Stucky's assignment foregrounds the body as a site of knowledge and becoming, which I believe is crucial for the development of critical thinking about difference, a focus close to the heart of many composition pedagogies. First-year writing textbooks regularly address questions of identity, difference, power, and social justice, all of which implicitly connect to how different embodiments—based, for instance, on race, ethnicity, class, gender, sexuality, disability, and so forth—shape social reality. Rather than studying emotioned bodies as textual features for analysis, a performative approach attempts to make physical the realities of being a certain kind of body in the world. This physical embodiment can augment, expand, and even transform understandings of what is behind textual representations of emotion, granting students access to emotioned investments that underwrite the surface of language.

Yet, I will not argue that emotion remains remote when accessed through textuality and thus that performative approaches are superior to textual ones. My intent is to suggest that we need a wide repertoire of choices governing how we teach emotional appeals and their stickiness. In particular, choices that make it possible to dramatize the relational aspects of emotional meanings and expressions provide teachers and students with a means for considering emotion as that which is in-play, between people, and situational—associations that have been long neglected by writing pedagogies. Also, the activities in this chapter indicate that the somewhat exaggerated meanings emergent from performative pedagogies are valuable because they insert play, physicality, movement, and seeing into writing classrooms, in effect stretching the concept of writing to include its ever-present materiality. While the materiality of writing occupies a good deal of scholarly interest, pedagogical illustrations and classroom enactments of materiality remain largely undeveloped, so that, perhaps unsurprisingly, teaching practices lag behind the exciting insights of scholarly research. In *The Wealth of Reality* (1999), Margaret Syverson describes materiality in a way that conjures its presence as the phantom limb of writing studies: "Neither writing nor reading can be accomplished without physical activity: clasping a book, moving the eyes across a line of text, using the muscles of the hand, arm, and fingers to handle a pen or keyboard....One of the salient features of academic life is the massive suppression of awareness of this physical relationship" (Syverson 1999, 12). The challenge, of course, is how to make physicality, with its attendant features of embodiment and performativity, a generative component of writing classrooms, rather than (only) a context for how we describe them. Here, then, are some attempts.

The exercise I sketch next requires preparatory large-group discussion about embodiment along the lines described in this chapter. Philosopher Mark Johnson's "Embodied Reason" (1999) is useful for this discussion, as he states persuasively why bodies matter for the study of knowledge, language, experience, and action. In this essay he links experiential possibilities to bodily realities: "What we can experience and how we make sense of what we experience depend on the kinds of bodies we have and on the ways we interact with the various environments we inhabit. It is through our embodied interactions that we inhabit a world, and it is through our bodies that we are able to understand and act within this world with varying degrees of success" (M. Johnson 1999, 81). In order to transfer this thinking to the claim that emotion is embodied, we could substitute emotion-words in Johnson's statement: "What we can [feel] and how we make sense of what we [feel] depend on the kinds of bodies we have and on the ways we interact with the various environments we inhabit" (81). Making explicit that emotions and bodies merge enables students to work with "the appeal to pathos" differently.

For this exercise, students read something relevant to an assignment that seeks to develop rhetorical skills. That is, I am imagining the following exercise will support a general focus on *getting* rhetoric—getting that language is an act with consequences shaped by and responsive to context, purpose, audience, and occasion. Getting also that rhetoric is more than the sum of these (and other) parts, a move that ranks the skill of identifying concepts below that of understanding how and why they are used as well as how one may use rhetoric's tools toward a desired purpose. This exercise helps students work toward a sense that rhetoric is capable of generating assent, attachment, and investment through means unavailable to analytical methods alone. How we come to be moved by language, images, and sound is messy and has much to do, as Johnson (1999) puts it, with the kind of bodies we have and how we inhabit the world.

Students assemble into groups of two or three to select a section of text from their reading that they think best exemplifies how and where emotion underwrites the surface of language or the emotioned sensibility of the piece. The passage need not be emotive in a conventional sense—using first-person, confessing a disturbing or moving truth, or writing directly about emotion—for, as I've suggested, economies of feeling are always in circulation, moving among bodies and objects, and generating attachment as well as detachment. Groups then decide which section of text to choose and once agreed upon, each group member brings into the following class-meeting a taped recording of him or herself reading the selected text aloud. In the same small groups, students listen to one another's taped readings and then talk through the differences or similarities in emphasis, voice intonation, and other features of notice. The goal is to generate conversation about the choices each person has made in the readings, the factors influencing those choices, and their effects. How does an oral reading open or close emotioned meanings? Inject emotion into the text in a particular way? Project certain characteristics onto the narrative/argument, characters/topics, or narrator/writer/theorist? As a group, students select features of the oral readings that they find most compelling in relation to the general spirit of the piece, and then one person is selected to read aloud and tape-record the selection again, integrating aspects of the readings that the group wants to preserve.

Students next practice performing the selected text in a manner that seeks to replicate the last tape-recorded version, with one or more students involved in the performance and one student assuming responsibility for directing (watching, assessing, and suggesting changes in the performance). In a subsequent class session, students perform their selections of the text for the whole class, culminating in a discussion, and possibly writing assignments, about how emotioned meanings are embodied—thus, messy and hard to locate and fix—rather than explicitly evoked to make an audience feel a certain way. Also, performing a text has the potential to nudge students out of an *interpret and/or analyze position*—a removed position "outside" the text—toward an *embodied position*, by which they are encouraged to make sense of what is written as a result of "interrogating other bodies through enactment" (Stucky 2002, 138). In its ideal form, this exertion in which students attempt to "share the breath" of the writer or a character may allow them to understand emotion through another's embodied reality. It can also add technicolor to the claim that emotion is in circulation by putting into play contrasting performances that differently emphasize aspects of emotion's work—its sticky hold on narrative, theory, or argument.

Thinking back to a recent section of advanced composition that I taught, I believe an exercise emphasizing emotion as performative and embodied would have enhanced my students' understandings of James Baldwin's *Notes of a Native Son*, excerpted in our textbook *Ways of Reading* (Bartholomae and Petrosky 2002). I am thinking particularly of my student Arielle McCoy's final reflective piece, in which she wrote that she came to Baldwin's essay with the assumption that he is "an angry black man that wrote things that hindered more than they helped" (McCoy 2004, 3). This statement illustrates the degree to which anger is a racialized emotion that sticks to black men, perhaps especially literary black men, so that they come to be associated with unjustified anger, particularly by white people. Locating anger *in* black men generally and, for my student, *in* Baldwin specifically, erases how anger is produced through cultural processes that include the transference of affect around understandings of race. The association between anger and blackness skirts Baldwin's depiction of the bitterness he feels, and that his father felt and passed on to him, as generational affect. Anger and bitterness are described in this excerpt as racialized emotions that are transmitted across generations; in Baldwin's world, both are part of a damaging inheritance. What propels the transference of bitterness in particular from one generation of black men to the next, Baldwin explains, is "the weight of white people in the world" (Baldwin 1955/2002, 54). He continues, "I saw that this had been for my ancestors and now would be for me an awful thing to live with and that the bitterness which had helped to kill my father could also kill me" (ibid.). The deathly serious aspects of the inherited emotions threatening to destroy Baldwin take the form of a "dread, chronic disease," characterized by a "blind fever" (ibid., 57). This chronic disease lies dormant and then flares up, has no cure, is all-consuming, and marks a person in an essential way—becomes an identity-marker and a fixed affect. Baldwin's contraction of the disease coincides with his first conscious realization of how racism operates and of his blackness as the source of others' hate, objectification, and dehumanizing treatment. Baldwin's characterizations of emotion as generational and linked to a chronic disease illuminate a powerful, pervasive transference of affect that is projected onto black male bodies.

McCoy's initial assumptions about Baldwin's unproductive anger are later replaced by her appreciation of his work's ability "to encompass everyone" (McCoy 2004, 3). She finds herself "struck by the emotion he was able to evoke and the way he made me think about what he had written" (ibid.) and includes the following passage, in which Baldwin writes about his relation to his father on the occasion of his death: "It was not that I had hated him and I wanted to hold onto this hatred. I did not want to look on him as a ruin: it was not a ruin I had hated. I imagine that one of the reasons people cling to their hates so stubbornly is because they sense, once hate is gone, that they will be forced to deal with pain" (Baldwin 1955/2002, 61). This reading of Baldwin as speaking a universal truth about the nature of hate and the hard-established connections to family characterized the students' readings on the whole, at the expense, I realize now, of attending to the production of racialized anger through a history of aggressive dehumanization of black bodies.

Facilitated and modeled by me, our text-based approach to reading, interpreting, and reckoning with Baldwin's narrative lacked the rigors of imaginative thinking that performative pedagogies elicit. For example, I wonder how enactment of emotions tied to blackness in this piece, attributed to Baldwin's father and expressed by Baldwin himself, would have animated a layered portrayal of generational transmission of emotion. A performance of both Baldwin's and his father's emotions, in other words, along with discussion about the choices embedded in these performances, might have called forth nuanced readings that go further to understand why readers might be "struck," to use McCoy's word, by "the emotion [Baldwin] was able to evoke." This approach might have also encouraged readings that bracket universal appeal in the work—"to encompass everyone"—in order to linger over the specificity of the father's and son's expressions of emotion in relation to racial oppression. I'm assuming, of course, that live enactment, including the study leading up to it and the discussion following it, changes our connection to text-on-the-page, gives it a new kind of dimensionality, and enables us to see relationships and story differently. Deep embodiment, or some version of what I have described earlier, opens us to experimentation with inhabiting, as much as possible, another's embodied emotions through an intimate relation to words as well as through a bodily-based performance of those words. It seeks to delve into the nuances and intricacies of cultivating a felt relation to the world different from one's own.

Students need not be acting majors or even skilled at performance in order to benefit from this exercise. On the contrary, bracketing movement and performance from the writing classroom for these reasons—the result of obstructionist disciplinary boundaries—closes off a whole range of activities that may stimulate the word-work and critical thinking that so many composition teachers hope to inspire. Deep embodiment pedagogy makes interpretation from the position of *what a text makes me realize about myself* unsatisfying, leading instead toward *what it is like to move around the world in a different body*. This movement from self as the source of knowledge and understanding to an affective projection and creative performance is one that significantly enhances and extends what we should do with emotion in the classroom.

Performance and Play

Performance inevitably shifts one's molecules and makes one new.
Joni L. Jones, "Teaching in the Borderlands"

In an effort to teach her performance students how to approximate the embodiment of an other, Joni Jones (2002) has developed a set of activities aimed at creating spaces in which students "play with cultural constructions" (Jones 2002, 177). Play is crucial for Jones because it is the ingredient that puts "theories of embodiment into practice" (ibid.). The exercises she has devised are geared toward developing a more acute, felt sense of others' experiences as well as an awareness of how each person performs in distinct, though usually unnoted, ways. The overall effect is to disrupt notions of an essential self and an essential other by foregrounding the role of performance in both constructions, which is potentially illuminating and disturbing. As Rinaldo Walcott (1998) writes in the context of performing black identities, "[E]very body performs, but only certain of these performances are noticed or read as such. Bringing into discussions, dialogues, and pedagogy the verbing of the noun, or rather the performance of performativity, signals a resistance to a static conception of identity, community, and politics" (Walcott 1998, 160–61). One exercise that Jones has developed to showcase the verbness of identity—identity as a state of becoming, change, and movement—involves a series of layered acts of representation and observation. Students write their names on pieces of paper along with adjectives that they see as opposite to their character, and then the class is divided into groups A and B. The sheets of paper from group A are given to group B. Here is what follows:

> Group A walks around naturally while each member of Group B closely watches the student whose paper they are holding. Group B is asked to take note of posture, eye contact, pace, angle of head, proximity to others, length of stride, and other performance features. Group A then performs the adjectives they wrote on their papers; Group B pays keen attention to the details of this performance. Group A is asked to sit, and Group B now begins to walk like the person they were observing. They also perform the assigned person's opposite, just as that person performed it. Students attempt to see themselves as performed by someone else. (Jones 2002, 179)

Following the exercise, class members discuss what it is like to perform and be performed by others. The context for this exercise is Jones' course, Performance of Dramatic Literature, in which, through acts of cross-cultural performance, "the classroom serves as a laboratory for the exploration of race and ethnicity" (ibid., 175).

Jones' ideas can be adapted productively for an exploration of emotion as a performative. As noted, a performative has the potential both to reiterate norms that support the status quo (how we identify ourselves) and to disrupt or challenge these norms (the opposite of how we identify ourselves). An emotion performative entails a bodily enactment, foregrounding emotions as things we *do*, rather than things we *have*. Along these lines, I am interested in using Jones' activity as a starting point for revising the application of Aristotle's appeals in writing classrooms. By having students perform and observe emotions linked to identity, we can generate new constructs for teaching the appeals, shifting our focus away from the idea that we *make* appeals and toward the claim that we *perform* them. Performing emotions suggests that emotions are not already *in* us or others, waiting to be externalized. It means that they take form, become recognizable, and enter the realm of rhetoric when they are bodily enacted and lived, which always entails some degree of performance. To generate liveness around emotion, as Jones' assignment does so well, creates opportunities for students to think through the ways in which cultures assign value and legitimacy to emotions through situated forms of expression. For example, sadness might be said to be *live*—not obsolete or dead—in the context of losing a family member. Sadness is more than a state of being in this situation; it is an emotive enactment that becomes recognizable through forms of expression such as crying, detachment from everyday life, sleeplessness, and so forth. By calling sadness a performance, I do not assert that it is somehow disingenuous or an "act," but that it becomes knowable through performances that are culturally recognized and sanctioned. Emotions are extralinguistic expressions that involve the body, cultural scripts, liveness, and, as Jones emphasizes, play. Using play to call our attention to performance as a central ingredient in identity formation and in perceptions of identity is to me one of the more compelling aspects of Jones' assignment.

The possibilities emergent from such an assignment may have provided fertile ground for students in a first-year writing class I taught several years ago, one that I occasionally revisit as I consider how to revise my teaching strategies. This class was particularly important to me because I saw it as an opportunity to integrate current events—the 2004 presidential election—into our study of writing and rhetoric, sensing that the presence of rhetoric and the role of writing leading up to the election could animate the rhetorical concepts that I wanted my students to employ in their own writing. I organized our course around civic participation in American culture. Using *Composing a Civic Life: A Rhetoric and Readings for Inquiry and Action* by Michael Berndt and Amy Muse (2004), I asked students to consider what democratic participation and civic identity meant for them. To facilitate this goal, we read and wrote about presidential candidates George Bush, John Kerry, and Ralph Nader, focusing especially on the rhetorical strategies employed by their websites, the scripts each candidate presented as central to their platforms, and the construction of voters made available through language use, argumentation strategies, and visual images. We also watched the presidential and vice presidential debates in class and discussed each candidate's demeanor and self-presentation in terms of rhetorical effectiveness.

For their first major paper assignment, students wrote what I called a *citizenship narrative*. In preparation, we read essays, in-

cluded in our text, by Benjamin Franklin, Ralph Ellison, and Anzia
Yezierska, in which the writers used narrative to depict civic life.
Representative excerpts that guided our discussion and preparation
for writing included the following:

Franklin on adding humility to his list of virtues:

> When another asserted something that I thought an Error, I deny'd my self
> the Pleasure of contradicting him abruptly, and of showing immediately
> some Absurdity in his Proposition; and in answering I began by observing
> that in certain Cases or Circumstances his Opinion would be right, but that
> in the present case there *appear'd or seem'd* to me some Difference, &c. I soon
> found the Advantage of this Change in my Manners. The Conversations I
> engag'd in went on more pleasantly. The modest way in which I propos'd
> my Opinions, precur'd them a readier Reception and less Contradictions;
> I had less Mortification when I was found to be in the wrong, and I more
> easily prevail'd with others to give up their Mistakes & join with me when I
> happen'd to be in the right. (Berndt and Muse 2004, 30)

Ellison's invisible man on invisibility:

> It is sometimes advantageous to be unseen, although it is most often rather
> wearing on the nerves. Then too, you're constantly being bumped against
> by those of poor vision. Or again, you often doubt if you really exist. You
> wonder whether you aren't simply a phantom in other people's minds.
> Say, a figure in a nightmare which the sleeper tries with all his strength
> to destroy. It's when you feel like this that, out of resentment, you begin
> to bump people back. And, let me confess, you feel that way most of the
> time. You ache with the need to convince yourself that you do exist in the
> real world, that you're a part of all the sound and anguish, and you strike
> out with your fists, you curse and you swear to make them recognize you.
> And, alas, it's seldom successful. (ibid., 32)

Yezierska, who emigrated to America from Russia, after finding
work in America:

> Now I had better food to eat. I slept on a better bed. Now, I even looked
> dressed up like the American-born. But inside of me I knew that I was not
> yet an American. I choked with longing when I met an American-born,
> and I could say nothing.
>
>   Something cried dumb in me. I couldn't help it. I didn't know what it
> was I wanted. I only knew I wanted. I wanted. Like the hunger in the
> heart that never gets food. (ibid. 41)

In the description of the citizenship narrative assignment, I encouraged students to develop a distinct "persona" and "tone" that
relayed their assumptions about citizenship, much as the writers
whom we read had done in their narratives. In retrospect, I think
what I was really hoping for, especially after reading the selections

by the three authors, was some exploration of what it feels like to be or want to be a "citizen" (or noncitizen, following Ellison) and what these feelings have to do with democratic participation. Or, if this is too much of an idealized revision, these are things I *should have been* interested in, about which students *should have* written. After all, the idea of membership, of belonging legitimately and legally, is saturated with sticky emotions about place, identity, detachment, belonging, and alienation. We see the stickiness around the idea of belonging in Benjamin's narrative, as he describes feeling less mortified when able to connect with people as a result of repressing his impulse to contradict them; in Ellison's depiction of the invisible man's resentment over being made invisible and his ache to feel differently; and in Yezierska's autobiographical piece, in which she relays longing, want, and hunger associated with becoming an American *on the inside*, not merely appearing to be one on the outside. These excerpts suggest that it is difficult, not to mention reductive, to bracket emotion from considerations of civic life, although this is effectively what I did when I substituted persona and tone, as does the textbook, for a directive that might have mined the affective stickiness underwriting these pieces.

In order to move students toward an engagement with emotion and citizenship, I would like to capitalize on Jones' foregrounding of play and movement in the classroom as a fertile basis for invention. That is, in my adaptation of her assignment, I highlight performance and play as inventional strategies for writing critically. Whereas I sketch an exercise specific to the citizenship narrative paper, a similar approach can be extrapolated for a wide range of assignments common in first-year writing classrooms. On a sheet of paper, students write their names followed by a short description of the form of citizenship they embody. Based on my students' explanations over the course of the term, these forms may include elements of social activism aimed at eliminating racism, boredom, apathy/indifference, consumerism, patriotism, cynicism, or a caring model of citizenship focused on improving the living conditions of the poor. The one caveat is that the description must in some way indicate the emotions associated with the form of citizenship identified so that, for instance, if a student describes citizenship as consumerism, the emotions associated with this position might include joy, numbness, denial, repression, or any number of other emotions linking consumption to being an American citizen. Below this description, students describe, very briefly, what they see as the opposite of that model of citizenship. The class is then split into two groups, and the sheets of paper are exchanged between groups with each student holding a sheet filled out by someone from the other

group. Next, students from group A walk around the class and perform—using gesture, posture, language, writing, facial expression,
and miming of activities, among other possibilities—the model of
citizenship that they identified as the one they embody. These same
students then walk around the room and perform the opposite
model of citizenship—again, through an enactment of how they
envision the antithesis of their own connection to citizenship. All
the while, students from the other group closely observe the per-
former whose name is on their sheet, trying to gauge the emotional
content of citizenship for that particular student and preparing to
emulate his or her performance. Students in group B go through
the same tasks while group A watches closely and also prepares to
emulate their partners. In the final round of performances, students
attempt to mimic their partners, imitating the others' performances
of citizenship and their opposites.

Once completed, students discuss their performances of self and
other—the difficulties, misrepresentations or accurate depictions,
intended and/or unintended effects, and skills required to observe
another without judgment. This conversation continues by focusing on the emotioned content of citizenship, the steeped affect that
informs concepts of citizenry and its associations with belonging,
place, legitimacy, and collective identity. Also, these issues may
evoke connections to democratic participation, a topic about which
students in my class were exceedingly animated and forthcoming.
When we read several web-based articles on the paucity of student
voters, for instance, I learned that nearly 75 percent of my students
planned *not* to vote in the upcoming election, a position that most
defended by saying that the issues in the campaign had nothing to
do with their own lives. Though I could not resist attempts to con-
vince them that policies regarding the declaration of war, health
care costs, and the future of Social Security intimately affect their
lives, a more rhetorically consequential approach might have been
to facilitate activities, like the one described here, to probe my
students' emotional investments in nonparticipation. Merely tick-
ing off logical explanations about why they should vote does not
amount to a learning experience or a particularly satisfying teaching moment, as impossible to ignore as the impulse may be.

Performance through play, by contrast, extends to students an
opportunity to see how, as Zembylas puts it, "emotions motivate
and accompany the performances of subjectivity" (in this case, the
subjectivity of citizen). At the same time, "emotions are constituted, established, and even reformulated by these performances"
(Zembylas 2003, 117). By emulating someone else's performance,
and performing one's own investment in citizenship, students may

see their positions, and the positions of their classmates, as in flux, as sites for thinking differently about how we develop and then fixate on ideas, actions, and ways of thinking. At the very least, we may have some fun with our students by getting people to move around, be "on stage," be an "audience," and feel the excitement—and for some, the dread—of being seen as a person with a body in a writing classroom.[4]

When Emotion Hijacks Critical Thought

What difference can a reconfigured rhetoric of emotion make to teaching highly charged, controversial material—material that seems to have an already built-in emotionality? This question has assumed difficult forms for me while teaching an undergraduate honors seminar entitled "The Culture of Eating Disorders," in which we examine the subject through an interdisciplinary framework that includes historical material, fiction and nonfiction narratives, feminist and cultural analyses, biomedical research, and psychological studies of patients with eating disorders. Students write short response papers, journal entries, and a final research paper on topics of their own choosing. The writing challenge for my students has been to transform emotional responses to the material into critical insights. Responses have ranged from empathy, anger, frustration, and suspicion to disgust and resentment of women's—and some men's—struggles with eating disorders. On the one hand, students have expressed a desire to understand better these illnesses and their causes; on the other, they have continually resisted understanding, charging the sufferers with vanity, willful self-destruction, and stubborn allegiance to sickness. These general responses have obstructed critical analyses of the material because, as students report, emotion seems to "get in the way" of analysis, leading to personal narratives that, in my view, neglect our texts and obscure the conflicts around causation that have emerged in our readings.

How do we complicate the construct of emotion as liability in an already highly emotioned site, where the feminized content seems to lead naturally to getting emotional? How do we reconceive emotion as a rhetorical resource—a source from which to draw out meaning, interpretation, and careful thinking? In order to question the seemingly natural link between the feminine and the emotional, my students and I talked about the tension between their emotional responses to the content and the analytical writing I expected from them. In the process, their interpretation of emotional responses as pure, honest, and true predominated. Their thinking was that the purity stems from an initial "gut reaction" to the material, a "natural" bodily response to what they were reading. Emotion, they argued, is unfiltered, unlike analysis, which takes form only after passing through the learned processes they have honed from writing numerous papers. I set out to complicate the idea that emotion is natural and reason is constructed; that emotion is real and pure, and reason is artificial and tainted. I did so by arguing that both modes are mediated by language and, in our case, by writing; thus, no pure, unconstructed representation of emotion or reason is possible. Even as we tend to think of emotion as emanating from a "first place," a kind of first response, there is a history, a social context, and a set of experiences that come to constitute that "first place." For my class, this history included a largely feminized construct of eating disorders and a general cultural resistance to understanding eating disorders as forms of mental illness, or as anything other than media-generated "problems." In terms of the social context that bears on our responses to the course content, our social world demands thinness and both abhors and finds fascinating, even admirable, the starving female body. Also complicating the idea of emotion as a "first place" is the set of experiences informing how women come to use their bodies and view other women's bodies as emotioned sites for transcribing an inner world onto the external surface of the body.

Next, I presented emotioned responses as central to critical analysis, not competing with it or emanating from a radically different place. Learning to see emotion as a usable resource, as grounds for doing rhetoric, is crucial if we are to trouble binaries that insist on planting reason on the side of decency and emotion on the side of shame. To this end, I asked students how their emotional responses could take a form other than personal narrative; that is, how can we use strong feelings as a resource for doing analysis, rather than regarding them as relevant only to personal writing, as appropriate for journaling but not for analyzing?

We read *Fasting Girls* (Brumberg 1998/2000), which details, among other things, the history of fasting female saints who understood starvation as a means for purifying the body and soul in service to God. One student wrote a response paper in which she accused the saints of being hypocrites more interested in their own image than the image of God; the saints were anything but holy and reverential to her—they were a disgrace. The anger this student expressed in her paper was palpable and seemed to emerge from her investment in a specific form of religious experience. Her response paper failed to deal with the saints on their own terms or to understand the world in which they were operating; instead, she used her contemporary value system as a way of reading the saints and their eating behaviors. Her emotioned perspective hijacked the history detailed in the book, holding it hostage to a belief system utterly incomprehensible within the context of female saints' lives. In conference, we talked about how her emotional investment in religious practice, and in what she takes to be an appropriate body construct, might be channeled differently, as a means, for example, by which to explore assumptions about the body and religiosity that informed the saints' concept of a spiritual act. In other words, we discussed the potential for using her emotional response to what struck her, what called her to write, as a guide for her engagement with the material. My goal was to encourage this student to use emotion as a basis for doing critical work rather than as a tool for moving an audience to do something or as the basis for *emoting*, an expression of feeling that speaks exclusively about the self.

This student conference led to a large group discussion about what to do with our emotions when attempting to write and analyze material overdetermined by emotionality. Our tentative thinking centered on an integrative approach that makes emotion an explicit part of our discussion of texts and reads emotion as an enabling invention-point, as a site for meaning-making and a potentially rich place from which to put words together. Our conversation led us to question our discounting of emotion as a credible and valuable resource for critical writing. This questioning was made even more relevant by the course material, which highlighted the persistence of the emotion/reason binary as seen through the body/mind split that has organized Western culture since at least Aristotle, for whom women were "mutilated males," emotional and passive prisoners to their bodies.

And yet, I can't say that these conversations produced discernible changes in my students' writing or in their thinking about interconnections between emotion and writing. Rather, when writing, students put their emotions in check, expressing caution about being overly emotional in their responses. Certainly not the result I had hoped for, but compelling evidence that talk and persuasion are not enough to shift what students and teachers do with emotion in the classroom. As I rethink my strategy from my current vantage point, it occurs to me that a performative approach to conceptualizing emotion would have brought my students closer to the breath of the writers, characters, and illnesses we studied. Because the body is the central site of contest and display for a person with an eating disorder, it seems obvious to me now that exclusively textual and analytical approaches simply cannot comprehend eating disorders and their varying representations without some way of accessing physicality. Also, an exercise modeling a way to experience embodiment differently would be useful in this course, in which the majority of students struggled to grasp, largely through rational, logical means, why someone might starve herself, binge and purge, engage in meaningless sex that leads to feelings of emptiness, and use drugs to feel numb. Logic fails when pushed against these realities.

Thus, a potential revision for addressing emotion in the context of eating disorders, or other highly charged, emotionally sensitive material, might include classroom activities that ask students to perform one facet of an illness, character, or author (as well as what they perceive to be an alternative characteristic) with a particular focus on the emotionality entailed in each performance. In an attempt to understand the anorectic lead character in *The Passion of Alice* by Stephanie Grant (1995), performing her emotional disposition and watching others perform it could lead to some valuable revelations that make this character more real, more than a character for whom we feel agitated or empathetic—that is, more than an object about which we feel something. Indeed, many of my students found Alice annoying because she is so emotionally unavailable to the readers. During discussion, her character became the object of dismissal before we really understood the experiences that motivated her seeming emotional lack. This dismissal was compounded by the fact that what Alice lacked in feeling, she made up for in her sense of superiority, an outgrowth of her reverence for anorexia: "My anorexia is a form of self-knowledge. [....] Anorexics differentiate between desire and need. Between want and must. Just to know where I begin and end seems, in this day and age, a remarkable spiritual achievement. Why relinquish that? Why aspire to less? Why assimilate?" (Grant 1995, 2).

Although many students complained about Alice's haughtiness, which they attributed to her frustrating habit of concealing her emotions from the reader and other characters, embodied performances of her emotional world might create a different relationship with Alice, one that makes contact with her character through understanding before judgment, personal beliefs, and other frames that close rather than open readings. Most importantly, though, performing Alice would mean having to understand her choices from *within* her world, organized, as it is, by rituals of deprivation and purification. I am interested in how improvising Alice through classroom activities might grant all of us in the classroom better access to how emotions stick to Alice and her anorexia. How can we get closer to understanding a world animated by drives for emptiness? Alice explains in the following passage that she has an "almost overwhelming urge" to tell her friend Ronald about the vast emptiness she feels, but instead she confides only in the reader:

> So I almost told him right then and there about the emptiness that the overeaters tried to fill with impossible amounts of food, again and again; the emptiness that the bulimics tried to disgorge, as if it had been caught, a chicken bone or a fragile green fish's gill in their quivering throats; the emptiness which we anorexics, in our superior knowledge and practice, tried to constrict, tried to compress by strangulation and deprivation, tried to irradiate with nothing, with time, with consistent daily loss [...]. (ibid., 240)

An interactive performance exercise might get students further involved in the characters' emotional worlds as well as in each other's interpretations of these worlds. For example, a small group of students might select a scene in the book in which emotional meanings are discernible, much as I described in the deep embodiment exercise above. Each group would perform its scene for the class without interruption. Then, each would perform it again, but this time other class members would stop the action when they see what they consider to be an act of misrepresentation or inaccuracy. At this point, a class member would enter the scene, excuse one of the original students, and then pick up the scene from that point, with the intention of injecting a changed affect into the scene. The group then would improvise from this point with the understanding that this is a form of play, experimentation, and spontaneity. The goal of this activity is to produce new understandings of the text and to test out alternative enactments that help to conceive the role of emotion as live and produced, not just *there*, in the characters, the illness, or any other object/circumstance. After each group's interrupted scene, the class would discuss the consequences of the intervention and its effect on our first responses and assumptions. In this way, emotion is shifted from its designation as a "first place" to a negotiable, fluid aspect of meaning-making that can and should be the object of critical thought, achieved through analytical as well as playful, performative, and inventive means.

This chapter is intended to get compositionists thinking about how to set emotion in motion in our writing classrooms in order to demonstrate that meanings associated with emotion are made and remade through varying bodily performatives. Just as we can work with students to engender a robust rhetoric of emotion that hinges on enactment, thus opening up a new way of seeing emotion effects in our reading and writing, we can also apply such a rhetoric to understand better the machinations of emotion discourse within our disciplinary scholarship, allowing us to identify the ethereal functions of feeling that shape professional identity. The next chapter follows this turn to disciplinary scholarship, extending my thinking about emotion as a performative by illustrating how emotion is enacted in the context of writing program administration, generating political effects that have often operated below the radar of composition scholarship, but that nevertheless have had significant impact on teacher efficacy and on configurations of academic work.

Notes

1. In Chapter Four I offer one interpretation of emotion's relation to working conditions, specifically for writing program administrators. Many studies addressing emotion and teacher identity and efficacy are available. Within composition studies, see Fontaine and Hunter 1993; Holbrook 1991; Schell 1998a. Researchers in education have also contributed significantly to this area of study; see Hargreaves 1994; Kelchtermans 1996; Nias 1996; Noddings 1996; Zembylas 2003.

2. Schechner, in "What Is Performance Studies Anyway?," narrates a brief but informative history of the field's formation and development. Although courses on topics now recognized as part of performance studies were being offered in the late 1960s, the field really became constituted as such in 1980 when the Department of Performance Studies was established at New York University's Tisch School of the Arts. For more on the development of the field, see Stucky and Wimmer's (2002a) introduction to *Teaching Performance Studies* (especially 12–16). On the relationship between performance and performativity, see Diamond's (1996) introduction to *Performance and Cultural Politics*.

3. I take these terms—imagination, inquiry, and intervention—from Conquergood (2002, 152). He describes performance through these activities as well as in terms of "creativity, critique, citizenship (civic struggles for social justice)" (ibid.). By theorizing performance studies as entailing both production and reception, his goal is to disturb the hierarchical division of labor in academic institutions between "scholars/researchers and artists/practitioners" (ibid.).

4. Certainly there are complications involved in asking students to perform in a nonacting classroom setting, including the fact that some students may be utterly fearful and resentful about being in front of others. I leave these complications undone here, trusting that teachers interested in adopting these exercises, or some version of them, will work within their local contexts—teaching constraints, student population, teacherly comfort-level with movement in the classroom—in order to do so.

Chapter Four

Disappointment and WPA Work

Previous chapters have outlined strategies for using emotion as an analytic that makes visible the circulation of affective meanings—meanings that may productively form the content of writing classrooms, as Chapter Three contends. This chapter argues that emotions have political effects as they accumulate and adhere to work locations. I illustrate this point through an analysis of disappointment in relation to writing program administration (WPA). The context of disappointment, as I understand it, is shaped by a number of overlapping factors, including but not limited to the following: the glut of job candidates in a saturated market; the increasing use and exploitation of adjunct teachers whose primary duty is the instruction of required first-year writing courses; and the general devaluation of the Humanities as a viable, socially relevant, and economically supportable enterprise. According to several recent critics, these conditions, especially the narrowing of the job market, have produced a distinct lackluster familiarity in the scholarship of English Studies. In his introduction to *Day Late, Dollar Short: The Next Generation and the New Academy* (2000), editor and literary critic Peter Herman notes that the next generation of scholars—by which he means critics at the beginning of their careers—are increasingly feeling "pressure to write not what we feel, but what we think we ought to say" (Herman 2000, 4). As a result, "a certain sameness starts to creep into scholarship, a certain predictability about conclusions, a certain reticence toward taking positions that might either lead to rejection at journals with considerable professional capital . . . or alienat[e] influential people and hiring committees" (ibid.).

The context for his discussion is theoretical knowledge, particularly the lack of new theoretical paradigms that would differentiate "next generation" scholars from their predecessors in the 1960s and early 1970s, the makers of Big Theory. Noting the intimate connection between research agendas and employment, Herman and his contributors elaborate the collapsing job market of "certain kinds" of literature jobs: "full-time, tenure-track jobs to teach upper-division and graduate level courses in literature, and in some cases, cultural studies" (O'Dair 2000, 47). Registering her disappointment about this turn in the market, contributor Sharon O'Dair refers to the alternative to teaching literature—the teaching of composition—as a "horrifying situation," a fate that "isn't fun or challenging or respected or rewarded" (ibid., 51). O'Dair boasts that she would rather write a "slacker dissertation" on slasher films, qualifying her for one or two jobs in the country, than write—good grief—"a dissertation on pedagogy in the composition classroom" (ibid.). Aside from the familiar detestation of teaching composition and the anachronistic view that composition scholarship is equivalent to a "dissertation on pedagogy," O'Dair's view illuminates an important facet of the culture of disappointment in academia: an exacting bitterness, or disappointed hope, in what the academy has become.

O'Dair is not alone in her view. We see a similar affect expressed within composition studies as well, although directed toward a different object. For instance, disappointed hope is central to Geoffrey Sirc's review (2001) of five recent books in composition studies. For him, these books evoke "a general sadness that the field has become materially impoverished, subsumed with a political simulation that has crowded out what I consider the poetic real: desire, beauty, joy, drama, struggle, and loss" (Sirc 2001, 518). Sirc adds, "My lingering sense, from reading these stories, is of a field that all reads the same books and shares the same notion of what counts as professional knowledge" (ibid.). Sirc critiques what he perceives to be a tired turn in the scholarly agenda of composition studies, a turn that, in his view, has generated an endless reproduction of "the political," forsaking the aesthetic elements of writing and reading. From very different perspectives, Herman and Sirc call our attention to a persistent market-driven reliance on the already said, the safe bet. They offer provocative touchstones for my focus on the culture of disappointment in the academy and its ever-widening scope.

Surely, disappointment in relation to working conditions and employment opportunities is one of the most familiar contexts for diminished hope and cutting cynicism among academics. We all know well-published scholars and talented teachers who are unable to attain a much-coveted tenure-track position, suspended in

agonizing limbo and existing on poverty-level wages. The response
to the job "crisis" has included advice on how to retool oneself
for life outside the "ivory tower" (Basalla and Debelius 2001; *The
Chronicle of Higher Education*), calls for halting the overproduction of
graduate students for nonexistent jobs, and activist efforts to union-
ize adjunct faculty in order to improve working conditions and gain
some semblance of career stability, including a livable wage (Schell
and Stock 2001). In addition, scholars across English Studies have
made academic work a significant object of study in itself (Bérubé
1998; Bousquet et al. 2004; Nelson 1997; J. Williams 1999). Just as
literary texts, language use, student writing, teaching issues, and
rhetorical and theoretical discourses have long occupied the making of knowledge in English, the nature of our work itself constitutes a growing site of intense focus.

WPA work has been especially scrutinized over the past ten
years. WPAs have become increasingly vocal about the disappointments entailed in administering writing programs with a lack of
support staff; in departments that fail to acknowledge the intellectual work required to develop curricula, syllabi, and teacher-
training courses; and in universities that generally neglect to count
these materials as fulfilling requirements for tenure. Current efforts
to professionalize WPA work, to argue for its legitimacy as scholarship and its necessity to a functioning undergraduate writing
program, have become commonplace. Precisely because WPAs are
arguing for their intellectual value to academic institutions, and
because they are working within the still devalued area of writing
instruction, they are the focus of this chapter. More specifically,
invested with the ostensible authority to design curriculum, hire
and fire writing instructors, serve on influential university committees, etc., WPAs seem to occupy a powerful location. The truth,
however, is that WPA authority and power is challenged, belittled,
and seriously compromised nearly every step of the way—a fact
that is compounded by the steady number of WPA positions ad-
vertised at the assistant professor level. WPA discourse provides a
telling case study, then, of how our profession inculcates affective
positions for WPAs. The target of all that woes student writing, the
target sometimes also of faculty in English departments who resist
rethinking, let alone changing, the way they teach first-year composition—WPAs find themselves immersed daily in anger, frustration, and disappointment (see especially George 1999). The typical
assistant professor in such a position has little power, yet he/she is
expected to be a quasi departmental business manager and to offer
some degree of guidance about writing instruction—although not
too much—to experienced faculty and other teachers in English and
across the disciplines.

There is a lively discussion going on in English Studies about administration in which WPA work has virtually no presence, a point I will return to in my concluding remarks. Rather than continuing to talk primarily among ourselves about the troubling working conditions for most WPAs, compositionists must begin to contribute to the larger dialogue on administration and to articulate WPAs' reality to a wider audience, those very people who have some stake in the way departmental faculty organize, define, and evaluate their work. An analysis of disappointment can be one basis for exploring the relationship between work practices and emotional dispositions that contributes both to the larger discourse on administration and to an understanding of those factors that create a culture of disappointment in the academy. Moreover, this analysis demonstrates that emotions *do* something besides express individuals' feelings, usually thought of as internal states; emotions function as the adhesive that aligns certain bodies together and binds a person/position/role to an affective state. These states become naturalized to the extent that they are not framed as problems but are viewed as inevitable and unchangeable; in effect, WPA work and disappointment are frequently conceived in such terms. My effort here is aimed at making this alliance a *problem* as well as suggesting strategies for combating this unnatural alliance.

I proceed by briefly outlining in the next section how compositionists have figured the relationship between their work, including WPA work, and emotion. The following section examines two recent WPA work narratives that foreground disappointment as a central affective component of the job. In the final section, I describe several implications of this study: the need to broaden the reach and impact of WPA scholarship, the advantages and effects of inserting emotion into materialist analyses of work, and the importance of educating ourselves about how work is organized in the university.

Figuring Work and Emotion

Critical reflection on emotion is not a self-indulgent substitute for political analysis and political action. It is itself a kind of political theory and political practice, indispensable for an adequate social theory and social transformation.
Alison Jaggar, "Love and Knowledge"

For quite some time now, compositionists have argued that the composition course and the pedagogies related to it reinforce dominant cultural values. Scholars have traced the means by which first-year composition has sought to reproduce class divisions in the culture at large and has trained students to join a stratified work-force (e.g., Crowley 1998; Gale and Gale 1999; S. Miller 1991b; Strickland 1998; Worsham 1998b). Miriam Brody notes in *Manly Writing* (1993), for instance, that the origins of composition courses in the late 1800s followed the Harvard model of theme writing. As a result, composition courses "decreed that some students' language was nonstandard, effectively disenfranchising nonelite linguistic communities and legitimizing the power and authority that already accrued to an educated and wealthy minority" (Brody 1993, 124–25). Brody's analysis, amplified by the work of countless others, has contributed to the politicizing of composition studies by showing its relation to dominant cultural machinery and its participation in oppressive social relations, even while many of its practitioners make claims for emancipatory teaching. The nature of this contradiction has generated a systematic examination of the political content of teaching and the profession more generally.

This examination has largely focused on economic dispari-ties within the academic work force (Enos 1996; Holbrook 1991), strategies for making heretofore marginalized discourses relevant to teaching practices (Campbell 2005; Gere 1994; Gilyard 1996; Jarratt 1991; Logan 1995; Powell 2002; Royster 2000), and peda-gogical methods for encouraging students to be active agents in the learning process (Fitts and France 1995; Giroux and McLaren 1989; Knoblauch and Brannon 1993). The political turn in compo-sition, however, has been slow to address the emotional contexts of teaching and learning. This perhaps has been due to the fact that emotion, up until very recently, has not been conceived as a social construct but, rather, as Michelle Payne states in *Bodily Discourses* (2000), as "outside culture, untouched by ideology, not subject to critical reflection" (Payne 2000, 11). On the whole, then, emotion has figured only minimally into accounts of student and teacher subject formation or classroom dynamics because it has not been thought of as having a social and political identity. A significant body of interdisciplinary work, however, suggests otherwise.

In "Understanding Emotions," psychologist Shula Sommers writes, "There seems to be a close association between cultural values and the emotional responses of individuals which, in turn, suggests that emotions need to be understood in terms of the rest of the culture and its ideology" (Sommers 1988, 31). The traditional psychological study of emotion—focused largely on individual emotional states—has broadened into examinations of how emo-tion meanings change across cultural contexts, making it possible to study the relationship between the emotional lives of individuals and the cultural systems that ascribe emotional meanings. This is the goal of Arlie Russell Hochschild's 1983 sociological classic, *The Managed Heart: The Commercialization of Human Feeling.* Studying the emotional labor of flight attendants, Hochschild argues that a major component in the services they offer involves selling an emotional experience to customers. The ever-present smile, Hochschild contends, is a provision of employment that is designed to sell "elation" to airline customers. The study reveals the often-contradictory relation between private and public acts of emotion, a relation that, because a good deal of emotional suppression is a condition of the job, often diminishes flight attendants' sense of self-worth and creative potential.

Hochschild's study makes clear that emotion is a highly gendered discourse: most flight attendants at the time of her writing were women, and the emotional labor expected of them—nurturing, supplying feelings of comfort, and generally affirming the emotional well-being of passengers—has been traditionally identified as feminine. The political dimensions of emotion, including gender ideologies associated with emotion work, constitute a significant area of emotion research (e.g., Bartky 1990; Lutz 1990; Ruddick 1984; Spelman 1989; Stearns and Stearns 1988). Alison Jaggar notes that Western epistemologies have largely pitted emotion against reason, associating emotion with "the irrational, the physical, the natural, the particular, the private, and of course, the female" (Jaggar 1989, 129). In her work, she seeks to show how emotion, like reason, is a vital component in the construction of knowledge and in the everyday activity of social life. Like Jaggar, other scholars convincingly argue that the interconnections between politics and emotion do not necessarily translate into psychologizing politics; instead, they can elucidate the ways in which emotional needs call forth political theories, institutions stunt or nurture political emotions, and ideologies of emotion injure people. They can also show us how a given cultural system produces emotional dispositions for its subjects. I explore this idea in the remainder of this section by outlining prevailing conceptions of work in the cultural system of composition studies and discussing how emotion figures into them. The purpose of this discussion is twofold: first, to show how the work we do in the profession has an affective dimension that is *not* outside politics or ideology; and second, to establish a relationship between work and emotion that provides context for my examination of disappointment and WPA work.

Work is one of the key processes through which we develop a sense of self-worth and potentiality. Analyses of work in composition and proposals for improving working conditions must address the fact that material satisfaction is only one function of work.

Marxist critics Samuel Bowles and Herbert Gintis (1976) explain that other functions include "social relationships among workers, and—most important—the development of the human potentialities of the worker as a social being, as a creator [...]" (Bowles and Gintis 1976, 69). They go on to claim that work has "a pervasive impact on the overall tenor of life" (ibid., 70). This includes emotional life and the process by which appropriate and inappropriate emotional dispositions, which are learned within institutional contexts, affect our work lives, scholarly activities, proposals for creating change in the academy, and our experiences as social beings in this profession.

Teachers are educated to adopt emotional dispositions that correspond to their place in academic and social hierarchies. In "The Costs of Caring" (1998a), for example, Eileen Schell explores the "workplace emotions" of part-time and non-tenure-track faculty members, finding that the emotional labor expected of them, particularly that involved with teaching and advising, forms a substantial basis for their exploitation (see also Schell 1998b). Moreover, she argues that compositionists' embrace of "femininism"—a pedagogy based on feminine values such as "nurturance, supportiveness, interdependence, and nondominance" (Schell 1998a, 76)—perpetuates gender ideologies that naturalize writing instruction as "women's work." "Femininist" values, she explains, offer feminists virtually no leverage with which to construct arguments that might challenge the continued exploitation of the largely female workforce of contingent writing teachers.

In *Gender Roles and Faculty Lives in Rhetoric and Composition* (1996), Theresa Enos reports that composition's "female ghettos" are characterized by gendered double-standards regarding tenure requirements, sexual and verbal harassment, unrewarded and unacknowledged administrative work by women, and an abundance of part-time adjunct positions staffed by women. Poor working conditions for contingent laborers and sexist workplace ideologies construct emotions as sites of social control. For instance, there is the tangible though often-unstated, sentiment that these teachers should feel grateful simply to have work, that excessive feeling about work inequities suggests an unearned degree of entitlement, marking one as a troublemaker who lacks respect for "the way things are." In addition, what can only be described as a free-floating frustration, hopelessness, and anger about working conditions is plainly detectable almost anywhere academics gather.

Affective dissonance is no stranger to WPAs. Most faculty beyond composition studies—and, indeed, some within it—assume that WPAs are administrators who simply *manage* writing programs as one would any institutional site. However, over the last ten years or so, WPAs have exercised considerable energy explicating the intellectual, scholarly knowledge, in addition to managerial know-how, necessary for their work (see Hult 1995; Rose and Weiser 1999; WPA Executive Committee 1996). In order to devise curricula, conduct teacher-training courses and faculty development workshops, establish a set of goals for a writing program, and determine assessment procedures, WPAs must have knowledge of the history and current status of writing instruction, including knowledge of key debates that animate WPA scholarship. In short, as Charles Schuster explains, unlike chairs, chancellors, and deans, WPAs "must possess both administrative skills and broad-based, up-to-date knowledge of highly specialized theory and practice" (Schuster 1995, ix).

The working conditions necessary for effective WPA work have been outlined in The Portland Resolution, a position statement articulated by the WPA Executive Committee and subsequently published in *WPA: Writing Program Administration* in 1992 (for a critique, see Gunner 1997). This document identifies professional standards for "effective administration of writing programs as well as equitable treatment of WPAs" (Hult et al. 2001). In a section entitled "Evaluating WPAs," the authors argue that assessment of WPAs should take into account the "scholarly contribution each WPA makes by virtue of designing, developing, and implementing a writing program" (1992, 89). The Resolution also addresses the material conditions necessary to do the job: "Resources include, but should not be limited to, adequate work space, supplies, clerical support, research support, travel funds, and release time" (ibid.). In addition, like other administrators, the authors state that WPAs require administrative support in the form of "clerical help, computer time, duplicating service" (ibid.). The Portland Resolution illustrates the extent to which WPA work is neither considered wholly administrative (warranting support staff and supplies) nor legitimately scholarly (warranting release time, travel funds, and so on). We can probably all agree that WPA work centers on the teaching of writing, but this simply does not adequately represent the range of expertise required for the job (see Janangelo and Hansen 1995; Myers-Breslin 1999; Rose and Weiser 1999). Unfortunately, the struggle to describe and legitimate the work that WPAs perform seems to be largely a case of WPAs talking to one another—the impact of this discourse beyond composition studies remains unclear. This point is emphasized when reading in the MLA *Job Information List* the countless ads seeking "managers" to handle everything from writing programs to writing centers to WAC initiatives, as if each area does not require specialized knowledge (after all, writing is writing—right?). In addition, such "super" manager positions often preclude time for meeting publication requirements necessary for tenure at most comprehensive, doctoral, and research institutions—a recipe for disaster for a beginning assistant professor.

The exploitation and delegitimization of WPAs and their work have been of particular interest to feminist compositionists, many of whom argue that, much like the teaching of composition, administering writing programs is largely aligned with women's work. In her 1995 study of WPAs, Sally Barr-Ebest found that "men fare far better than the women. They publish more, they are paid more, and they are more likely to be tenured" (Barr-Ebest 1995, 53). A good portion of the difficulty for women is the emotional labor— "feeding egos and tending wounds," to use Sandra Bartky's formulation—that they are either compelled or expected to perform. Barr-Ebest includes a sampling of responses from male and female participants who, among other things, discuss the gendered way that emotion work tends to play out among WPAs:

> Women are expected to do more—to be mothers to unruly staff members—to listen to men talk about their embarrassing personal lives—to always be polite and accommodating.

> Many of us take on greater responsibility than our male colleagues, especially if we bring feminist principles to our work lives (e.g.—valuing collaborating; working closely with grad students, etc.)." (ibid., 66)

Barr-Ebest's research suggests that emotional labor in the context of WPA work is not merely the private act of caring for and supporting others; much like Hochschild's flight attendants, female WPAs manufacture a product that benefits the business of academia. The benefit lies in the way in which affective production reinscribes women as nurturers whose job involves the unpaid labor of nurturing others. The sex/affective production involved in WPA work entails the production and reproduction of people (i.e., teachers) through processes akin to parenting. Engaging in this kind of domestic work in both private and public realms is a learned emotional habit for which women in capitalist culture are rigorously schooled (see Ferguson 1991; Rubin 1995/1990). The costs, as Eileen Schell demonstrates, include the devaluation of the work that women do by marking it as "women's work"—not serious, rigorous, or intellectual but rather, consistent with dominant views of composition studies, namely, service-oriented and practical.

Feminists have also critiqued what has been called the WPA-centric model of work, which envisions the ideal WPA as one who maintains centralized power over the writing program (Bloom 1992; Olson and Moxley 1989; White 1991). In "Decentering the WPA," Jeanne Gunner (1994) argues that this model contributes to professional status problems for writing specialists by perpetuating the "traditional power relationship that exists between the WPA and writing instructors" and creating a division between teachers and curriculum thereby "minimizing the role that all faculty should play in program direction" (Gunner 1994, 8). Gunner presents a model of decentered WPA work consisting of rotating positions and faculty committees (see also H. Miller 1996). Marcia Dickson (1993) also proposes a decentralized model through the creation of feminist administrative structures. As she describes it, this model would entail a WPA's willingness to "relinquish control over the word," collaborate, diversify authority among participants according to ability rather than rank, experiment with activities related to teaching and research, support and mentor participants, and develop a reward system for "excellence and effort" (Dickson 1993, 152).

Much WPA scholarship reads like a cautionary tale, expounding how not to get discouraged, burnt-out, manipulated by faculty and deans, and turned down for tenure. On a more positive note, it also includes much discussion of the rewards and pleasures entailed in teacher training, collaborative work, and other aspects of the job that create a community of teachers committed to providing quality writing instruction. In other words, emotional ambiguity seems a staple component of the experiences that WPAs narrate in print, online, and in person. This ambiguity was apparent to me when I solicited, via WPA-L, responses to a survey on affect and work in 2002. I received twenty-one responses from individuals in a variety of positions, including tenure-track and fixed-term directors of writing (including Basic Skills and Developmental Writing directors), directors of writing centers, a director of graduate studies, a director of undergraduate studies, teaching assistants, and tenure-track professors. The respondents worked at four-year research and comprehensive institutions, small liberal arts schools, and, in one case, a community college. In their ranking of the frequency of emotions experienced in their work lives, the respondents identified, from a list that I provided, disappointment, frustration, enthusiasm, empathy, and joy as the most prominent (in that order). This ranking suggests to me the wild range of emotions that result from doing interesting, often challenging work while being engulfed in a frequently emotionally dysfunctional relationship with an institution. The seemingly constant need to defend the purpose, goals, and outcomes of writing programs to faculty across the disciplines, to upper-level administration, and increasingly to state assessment boards is coupled with the knowledge that, as one respondent put it, the job "involves making people unhappy much of the time—telling them they cannot do something, denying a schedule request, having to explain why they received a poor observation report." Yet, rather than casting their duties in terms of emotional disempowerment, the respondents tended to characterize emotion as a politicized expression that WPAs must draw on carefully and purposefully, as the following examples illustrate:

> I think expressions of emotion . . . should protect students and colleagues who have less power than I, or who could suffer if I expressed, for example, frustration or anger.

> I work hard at making compassion the focus of my work as an administrator and it helps me to avoid rage, anger, etc., for instance when one of the faculty is blaming me because the lab has a virus and his life isn't going smoothly. That happened today. Which reminds me I need to send a message saying the computers should be fixed by next week. The virus got onto a big multilab network.

> My perception that I can make positive change produces a certain amount of enthusiasm that keeps me active. My anger also can propel me, as I'll stay in the office longer, trying to figure things out.

These comments suggest the inextricable link between expressions of emotion and the politicized institutional locations from which WPAs work. For them, emotion *produces* something—it is itself a kind of work that disables change, and less commented upon, also enables change through purposeful deployment. In addition, respondents articulate an awareness of how their positions of relative power enable them to direct the energy of a so-called "negative" emotion such as anger toward problem-solving, while they also reveal awareness of how controlling their own emotions is key to preserving relationships and protecting subordinates.

Using emotion to create change, as in the last example of the administrator who motivates himself through anger, characterizes several respondents' understanding of their own participation in emotion management. For instance, one administrator writes that she has "learned how important it is to be nice to people, listen to their issues, and try to talk them through any extreme emotions. . . . [E]motional balance and empathy come into play here." Another admits that he spends much of his time "managing the consequences of others' indifference to all that writing could be." He goes on to say that "nearly everything I do here is prompted by anger, anger at how the larger profession lets so many things get in the way of developing our nascent understanding of how writing and rhetoric are best learned."

Inherent in the above descriptions is the long-standing tension between the teaching and administering of writing and the larger professional attitudes about writing that WPAs regularly face. In this sense, the emotional dispositions that seem to accompany administrative work involve what Debra Meyerson calls *toxic leadership* (2000). This term refers to leaders who "act to absorb, dispense and dissipate pain and suffering in a system—people whose efforts require extraordinary acts of courage and compassion" (Myerson 2000, 173). The WPA who listens empathetically to others' issues, talking people through "extreme" emotions in an attempt to dissolve or alleviate them, and the WPA who deals with the consequences of others' indifference to writing are examples of toxic leadership at work. It is important to note that toxic leadership happens in a social system and emotional environment marked by intersubjectivity; it is, in other words, "a product of the way systems of meaning are created and negotiated *between* people" (Fineman 2000, 2; my emphasis). Understanding emotions as intersubjective processes invites us to consider the emotion management carried out by WPAs as more than an art of suppressing personally felt and systemically nurtured "negative" emotions. It is also a means for constructing an emotional culture around writing that acknowledges the familiar obstacles and tensions and that absorbs toxicity in an effort to provide leadership in support of innovative pedagogical practices.

The emotional management and toxic leadership of WPAs is not merely a generic feature of managerial pressures. The distinctiveness is due, in part, to writing itself being an extremely emotioned arena. From "Why Johnny Can't Write" to "Students' Right to Their Own Language," from Standard English debates to regular complaints from everybody and their neighbor about the lack of skill among student writers, there can be no doubt that the subject of writing ignites emotions in a stubborn, predictable, and sometimes infuriating way. The paradox, of course, is that highly emotioned and politicized discourse about writing as central to student learning aligns uncomfortably alongside metaphors that emphasize the devalued status of writing instruction: "sad women in the basement," "freeway flyers," and so on.

As several teacher-responses to my survey attest, the emotioned history of composition studies actively weighs down on day-to-day activities. One teacher who rated frustration as a frequently experienced emotion said, "I think the frustration comes from the feeling that I cannot effect change, both in the profession and at times, in the lives of my students. I wonder if what I'm doing has value. I wonder if students benefit from my teaching and I wonder if I'll ever feel that the work I do is rewarded." Another wrote, "'Frustration' and 'loneliness' work together in my work life. I'm the ONLY rhet/comp specialist on my entire campus—though of course everybody in the English Dept. (and many beyond it) thinks they're experts on writing pedagogy. Much frustration emerges from a general lack of understanding of what rhet/comp (and real writing pedagogy) is all about, combined with a superior attitude toward me."

These comments reveal that quality writing instruction is threatened by adverse working conditions and by the morale of the workplace. I explore this idea further in the next section as I focus on the limitations imposed by the affective experience of disappointment and the strategic ways in which WPAs use disappointment as a framework for effecting change, however compromised and tempered such change may be. My discussion of disappointment as a central emotional disposition of WPAs will comment on how academic institutions function at the affective level to generate loyalty, create perceptions of good workers, and suggest what workers should be willing to contribute to the professional community. These functions assume that emotions express attitudes and beliefs held in common by community members and that, as vital components in social relations, they are intertwined with issues of power and status in the work world.

Two Narratives

Writing about his experiences as a WPA, Richard Miller, in "Critique's the Easy Part," describes the need to cultivate "'the arts of contending with disappointment' for surely, there is nothing so dependable in this line of work as disappointment, rejection, defeat" (R. Miller 1999, 7). The WPA must navigate the murky waters of institutional hierarchy where decisions to create any sort of change are seriously constrained; where daily existence requires pragmatic, sometimes morally problematic decisions, and where one's ability to act on one's conscience or political ideals is seriously compromised. As stated earlier, the WPA occupies a paradoxical location: although he/she would seem, on the surface, to have a significant amount of power, Miller makes clear just how compromised that power is. As a result, the affective element that Miller characterizes as most common in his professional life is disappointment. He writes,

> Get disappointed enough times, see two or three carefully thought out plans go down the drain and cynicism and despair seem like the only reasonable responses to have. And, once one has fallen into that mindset, all

that's left to look forward to in the long walk to retirement is a life spent letting everyone else know that everything in the system works together to prevent innovation. That change isn't possible. That hope is for the young, the naïve, the foolish. (R. Miller 1999, 8)

Miller neither offers strategies for transforming the inevitable disappointment and despair into a more productive resource for professional survival nor argues for needed changes, constructs goals for restructuring our work, or outlines a utopian ideal that might begin to address the learned disaffection that underscores our work. Instead, Miller writes that WPAs must be able to translate their moral outrage about inequities and wrong-headed policies into economic terms, a language that deans can appreciate and understand. Miller makes available to us a clear example of the affective context of the work of WPAs and academics more generally. In sum, he contends that WPAs must choose to act in the face of despair and hopelessness, knowing full well that the changes one would most like to implement may never come to pass. With this knowledge in hand, Miller says, WPAs must act out of "the information at our disposal, our guiding principles and, perhaps, some inexplicable intuition about which way to turn" (ibid., 13).

What is politically necessary, from Miller's perspective as a wizened WPA, is to learn how to act in the face of disappointment in order to get something done. His suggestions are not, as it might seem, to resign oneself to circumstances that overshadow one's ability to function, but rather to develop a rhetorical understanding of work contexts, including an understanding of the language one must use to survive as a WPA. For Miller, rhetorically positioning himself as a WPA requires an ability to use language as a practical activity aimed at making small inroads on behalf of writing instructors and students. Rather than deny the context of disappointment that circumscribes his work, Miller emphasizes the need to make choices, especially when those choices are compromised by institutional limits. By articulating the reality of negative experiences that frequently structure our work lives (whether or not we are WPAs, I would argue), Miller develops a multilayered description of academic work. This description is useful because it shows that an affective context circumscribes how we work—how we function on a daily basis, how we envision the possibility of creating changes, and how we develop a sense of efficacy and purpose in our work lives. To deny the negative emotional realities of the academy does a disservice to faculty and the graduate students we train, for it leaves all of us unprepared to navigate our way through the material, including the affective realities of academic life (see Tompkins 1996).

In *The Importance of Disappointment* (1994), psychologist Ian Craib explains the denial of negative experience in a context wholly distinct from academia. He discusses this denial by health professionals, who respond to the wider culture of emotional control (see Lutz 1990 on women and emotional control; Stearns 1986 for a history of emotion management). Craib writes,

> The cultural pressures, often normal pressures which have to do with wanting to help people, to ease suffering, to be effective, to be good at our jobs, make us vulnerable to the denial of the necessity and inevitability of certain forms of human suffering. We set out to cure and we construct blueprints of what people *ought* to be feeling, *ought* to be like, and we can too easily set about trying to manipulate or even force people into these blueprints. (Craib 1994, 8)

Craib goes on to argue that modern culture's turn toward emotion management by experts denies the importance and validity of disappointment as well as other negative emotional experiences (see especially Chapter 5). He notes that, on the one hand, our culture has created an illusion of one's power, making "the reality of disappointment harder and harder to countenance" (ibid., 82); on the other hand, the ability to talk about one's emotions, rather than act on them, has amounted to an obsession with emotion management (ibid., 88). The seemingly endless supply of self-help books on handling anger, surmounting sadness, and discovering 101 ways to be happy, in addition to the emotion experts who regularly appear as mediators on afternoon talk shows, demonstrate the prominence of the cult of emotion management in American culture. The message to be inferred from this attention to harnessing one's emotions is that they can and should be controlled. Conceptualizing emotions as things to be "worked through," in an ongoing attempt to reconstruct ourselves and our relationships, has produced what Craib calls "the myth of self-control and of the all-powerful self that can control itself" (ibid., 117). This myth cannot account for the constraints on decision-making familiar to most WPAs or for the necessity to act in circumstances in which one has little to no control. WPAs and other academic workers function in what Susan McLeod, drawing from Patricia Ashton's research on teacher motivation, describes as a "mesosystem" (1997), which is characterized by "the general climate of the department and the institution, collegial relations, and relations with the administration" (McLeod 1997, 119). This "climate," McLeod explains, shapes teachers' sense of efficacy and their relationship to their work and workplace. The mesosystem determines how we position ourselves in relation to our work; it determines what we learn to see as changeable and unchangeable. In this sense, our work is shaped by both the material conditions of our labor—money, decision-making power, and teaching and administrative responsibilities—and the affective mesosystem that frames these conditions.

Mara Holt (1999) exposes and problematizes the often insidious workings of the mesosystem in "On Coming to Voice," which, like Richard Miller's essay, appears in Diana George's edited collection, *Kitchen Cooks, Plate Twirlers, and Troubadours: Writing Program Administrators Tell Their Stories*. Holt begins her narrative by discussing her emotional and intellectual disconnection from her work, which emerged in full force after attaining tenure. Asked by the current director to take over as director of composition, Holt needed time to think before accepting the position. She writes, "I was exhausted from the tenure process. Wounded. Crazy from having kept my mouth shut for the previous year and a half, just in case I might inadvertently plant some malice where it could unconsciously sabotage me. I was developing physical symptoms of stress that I'd never seen any sign of before. I was more angry than I ever remember being, and frightened to act" (Holt 1999, 27). Referring to Audre Lorde's writing on the connection between work and pleasure, Holt describes the dissonance she experienced between her emotions and her work: "I had suppressed my feelings, my motivation for work had become problematic, and I was angry" (ibid., 27).

Although she had not yet agreed to assume the administrative post, Holt details the mounting responsibilities that she assumed as a sort of de facto WPA—teaching the TA training course, acting as a teaching advisor, and explaining and justifying the writing program policies that she had no part in creating. Her service responsibilities, as many might imagine, came to threaten hard-learned lessons in graduate school—namely, that gaining a foothold in the profession requires significant research and publication. The difficulty of reconciling these competing demands on her time and energy amounted to a level of professional alienation that is probably familiar to many of us. She writes, "I had such faith in the appropriateness of my insecurity in the unpredictable world of English Studies that even my successes made me suspicious"(ibid., 35). In addition, while the raw ambition and competitiveness of graduate school had prepared Holt for the hierarchical and sometimes emotionally violent nature of academic culture, she reacted by silencing herself, losing confidence in her ideas and her legitimacy in the profession.

Feeling privately fearful and professionally lost, Holt was expected to identify with her home university by serving as the director of composition. As is the case in capitalist culture more generally, loyalty to the institution and its needs outweighed, actually made irrelevant, Holt's personal and professional needs. Yet her ability to function as an academic worker was intimately tied to the affective contexts shaping the social relations of the profession. Holt experienced alienation from her work as a result of feelings of powerlessness, isolation, and self-estrangement. Alienated labor, Marx explained, is first of all labor that is "external to the worker, i.e., it does not belong to his essential being; that in his work, therefore, he does not affirm himself but denies himself, does not feel content but unhappy, does not develop freely his physical and mental energy but mortifies his body and ruins his mind [...]. External labor, labor in which man alienates himself, is a labor of self-sacrifice, of mortification" (Marx 1844/1963, 110–11). Labor produces people, thus their sense of efficacy, potentiality, creativity, and meaningfulness is intrinsically connected to the nature of work. In particular, the unique situation of WPAs in the academy involves a form of emotion management that enhances and affirms the emotional and professional well-being of others often to the neglect of one's own emotional stability. Because the work of administering writing programs involves various kinds of personal and professional support—mentoring teaching assistants, cooperating with institutional writing initiatives, functioning as a sounding board for student and faculty grievances—emotion management is a significant portion of the job.

The disappointments that Miller and Holt express are inevitably connected to hope and the experience of disappointed hope. Hope, psychologist William Lynch has written, "is always imagining what is not yet seen, or a way out of difficulty, or a wider perspective for life or thought" (Lynch 1965/1974, 23). Lynch continues, noting that hope not only imagines, "it imagines *with*" (ibid.). That is, in his understanding, hope is an act of mutuality—an act of collaboration between members of a community. It is collaborative in the sense that one's vision for what might be is within the realm of *the possible* in a given community. Disappointment, in contrast, develops from a sense of hopelessness stemming from *the impossible*, or from what is made to *seem* impossible. From this perspective, disappointment is a failure of imagination nurtured by material conditions as well as by diminished faith in others. The personal and professional danger of disappointment is that it may become a "fixed" stance, eventually hardening into disillusionment, resignation, passivity in the face of new, ever-changing situations.

A central part of the context in which disappointment in academia develops must be the loneliness that academic life inevitably breeds. Whether this loneliness derives from the fact that we must go where the jobs are—often situating us far away from family and friends, not to mention airports that would take us to them—or that we may be the only compositionist (or theorist, multiculturalist, feminist, and so on) in a department, or that we find ourselves working in departments where not all voices count equally, it is clear that academia can be an extraordinarily lonely place. Loneliness is also arguably a predictable consequence in a profession that, despite rhetoric to the contrary, privileges single-authorship, cultivates fierce competitiveness, and establishes a dichotomy between research and practice, pitting teaching against "our own work."

Loneliness, however, is more than a physical place that we occupy. It can describe the relations we build, or fail to build, with others—especially those with whom we do not agree or whom we view as occupying a place of such remote difference that any relation seems impossible. Sometimes, in the name of self-preservation and principled thinking, loneliness must be *chosen*. In her influential essay, "The Master's Tools Will Never Dismantle the Master's House," Audre Lorde (1984) comments on the strategic necessity of choosing loneliness. She notes that survival means "learning how to stand alone, unpopular and sometimes reviled, and how to make common cause with those others identified as outside the structures in order to define and seek a world in which we can all flourish" (Lorde 1984, 112). In Lorde's view, choosing to stand alone and differentiate one's position from existing ones—too often perceived as solidified commonplaces beyond question—is sometimes necessary in order to effect change. The difficulty of this position has to do with the inevitable loneliness that comes from standing alone, "unpopular and sometimes reviled." Such positions easily invite our superiors to make our lives difficult on both the daily level of teaching and the institutional level of attaining tenure, securing grants, and serving on influential committees. Yet choosing loneliness may sometimes be the most viable and ethical response to disappointment in that it can allow an individual to be actively and politically engaged.

Although *choosing* loneliness can be a political strategy and a form of self-preservation, *participating* in a politics of loneliness that denies difference can engender disconnected relations between self and other. I refer here to a loneliness that refuses to acknowledge people-not-like-me and rejects different ways of thinking about knowledge, teaching, hiring practices, and so forth. In Lynn Worsham's formulation of whiteness as a politics of loneliness, she describes "a loneliness so profound that, in refusing to recognize and respect difference, it has never truly admitted the possibility of other people" (Worsham 1998a, 341). In addition to this profound refusal to acknowledge difference, an academic politics of loneliness also fails to admit changing realities that circumscribe our work and new ways of thinking that these changes require. As such, there is a tendency to resist change, perhaps because suggestions for change are always met with suspicion and fear of setting new precedents from which there is no turning back. The ability to have hope for the future of our profession requires us to demythologize the politics of loneliness by seeing ourselves in connection, rather than in distinction, to those we learn to see as outside the parameters of our work lives. Loneliness can function as a seedbed for disappointment, the experience of feeling dispossessed of power, agency, and the capacity to make a difference. It is not only common to experience disappointment in academia or to witness the disappointments experienced by those around us, but also to become *accustomed* to, even to *expect*, disappointment so that intervening in the conditions that create it often becomes unthinkable. We must begin to think more about how disappointment is woven into the fabric of our work lives and how we can combat destructive disaffection by improving working conditions, a goal that will in turn improve the education that we provide to students.

Implications

During the initial drafting of this chapter in 2000, I began to find examples of disappointment everywhere I turned: my students' writing, my teaching abilities, my department, the proliferation of high-stakes testing as a gauge for "learning" in public schools, and, most vividly, the presidential election process. Al Gore, in his concession speech, addressed disappointment directly: "I know that many of my supporters are disappointed. I am too. But our disappointment must be overcome by our love of country" (Gore 2000). Fearing that admission of disappointment might weaken international perspectives on the American democratic process, Gore continues: "And I say to our fellow members of the world community: Let no one see this contest as a sign of American weakness. The strength of American democracy is shown most clearly through the difficulties it can overcome" (ibid.). Quick to recover any sense of loss and hopelessness that his comments might betray, Gore configures the "difficulties" of the election process as notable because they are finally "overcome." Gore aligns Americans' ability to overcome difficulty with patriotism and the unshaken dominance of the United States. To linger too long on what was disappointing about the election would be to reveal weakness and enduring difficulty. Just as disappointment is, in the context of political life, what Jaggar (1989) calls an "outlaw emotion"—inappropriate and thereby threatening to the order of things—it also occupies an inappropriate (although not invisible) space in academic life. Not only does the admission of disappointment make one vulnerable, but it also threatens to construct one as a whiner, a disrupter of the status quo, and an ungrateful worker in the profession. Yet as Miller and Holt's narratives demonstrate, disappointment is a very real affective component in our work lives. In my concluding remarks, I outline several implications that emerge from my reading of disappointment's adherence to WPA work.

1. *We need to engage in a broader dialogue about administration.* WPA scholarship can contribute an important and much-needed perspective on administrative practices, especially in terms of feminist critique and collaborative administration. We see the need for a more nuanced discussion about administration in a recent cluster of articles in the *ADE Bulletin*. For Barry Sarchett (2000), the possibility of enacting political change from an administrative post is so alluring that he can not fathom why, when he and his fellow panelists delivered their papers on "Administration after Poststructuralism" at the 1999 MLA Convention, a "prominent feminist scholar" in the audience admitted that she had recently turned down an opportunity to become dean. Offended by the "feminist objector's" implied charge of political co-optation that accompanies administrative work, Sarchett counters that "crucial political issues" can be pursued from just such a position (Sarchett 2000, 1). As he reflects on the panelists' papers and introduces them to readers of the *Bulletin*, Sarchett remarks, "The panelists felt that in administrative posts they could be most effective in implementing policies to their tastes (and to mine, incidentally)— policies, strangely enough, that seemed to support the political agendas one might reasonably infer would be shared by the feminist objector. Why, therefore, wouldn't she embrace the chance to move into administration?" (ibid., 2). Imagining he knows the effects of the feminist's choice, Sarchett continues: "Inevitably, our feminist resistor had already compromised herself by resisting the move into administration. By making a judgment that she will be more effective outside administration, she has compromised her potential ability to affect policy more decisively within it" (ibid.). Although the, no doubt, numerous reasons why "our" feminist objector turned down a deanship are unknown to me (and to Sarchett, for that matter), that is not really the story here. The real

story is about Sarchett and his "administrative desire," as he calls it, to create an academic world in his own image, one that suits his taste. If the feminist objector fails to see the political power available through a deanship, then Sarchett claims that she is self-absorbed and overly concerned with "her own politics" rather than "the political success of her actions" (ibid.). At the same time, Sarchett emphasizes that he enjoys his position as dean precisely because he can use it as a vehicle for implementing policies to his own tastes—a vehicle for *his own politics*.

What apparently escapes Sarchett is that not all deans are created equal (see also Morris 1981, especially Chapter Two, "The Administrative Temperament"). Whereas he may feel no trepidation and experience no resistance to wielding power from behind a dean's desk, others may feel vulnerable in such a position. I do not pretend to know the feminist objector's specific concerns about political co-optation, but it is clear to me that women have a more conflicted relation to wielding power in administrative posts. Feminist WPAs, for instance, tend to characterize themselves as members of collaborative teams rather than as single agents of academic change. Without pretending that such collaborative arrangements are perfect (see Goodburn and Leverenz 1998), feminists resist models of administrative work that centralize power into one individual. In contrast, Sarchett and one of his co-panelists, Stanley Fish, conceive academic administrators as figures who work alone to get things done. In the best example of disappointment and academic work that I could find, Fish announces, in "Nice Work If You Can Get Them to Do It" (2000), the uselessness of poststructuralism to the lives of administrators, the futility of "high ideals," the impossibility of exercising context-specific prudence, and the final truth about administrators: "they are bound to fail" (Fish 2000, 4). "No wonder administrators have a shorter shelf life than NFL running backs," quips Fish, "it is only a matter of time before you zig when you should have zagged, and you are thrown for a loss from which you cannot recover" (ibid.). Unlike his analogy to a running back—whose position only has meaning in the context of a team—Fish's characterization of being a dean is a solidly solitary one. This is not to suggest that deans are not, in the end, the ones who are responsible for initiatives pursued under their leadership, for surely this is how things work. But, even when they act, they do so, most often, after conferring and debating with others—they talk with faculty, other administrators, and possibly students in order to determine a course of action. WPA scholarship provides tools for challenging an administrative model that privileges the "man of action" model as well as for complicating notions of power that, like Sarchett's, assumes that everyone wants it, can use it to advance a political agenda, and can wield it equally. WPA scholarship also provides many examples of the gendered nature of administrative work and the emotional labor it entails. When I began researching scholarship on general academic administration, I was struck by the overwhelming number of male-authored books. The startling lack of female researchers in this area speaks volumes about the gender politics of administration—a point that deserves analysis from feminist scholars in particular (for an exception, see Kolodny 1998).

In addition to the critiques that WPA scholarship can bring to bear on administrative work more generally, the dialogue on academic administration can broaden the implications of WPA research. For instance, WPAs may benefit from contextualizing their arguments for fair work practices into a larger discussion about administration. Such a move might be more persuasive to deans and chairpersons as they negotiate job offers for WPAs. I think especially of the need for basic resources—such as access to a copy machine, support staff, and adequate office space—that many WPAs must go without because of a lack of understanding or an aggressive inattention to the working conditions of those who administer writing programs. Studies of academic administration provide a rich context in which WPAs might situate their arguments for improved working conditions as well as a vantage point from which to see connections across the administrative spectrum. Because I have been discussing disappointment and WPA work, for instance, note the similarities to WPA work narratives in the following descriptions of administrative work by former deans and chairpersons:

> [While pleased with my progress as dean], I also knew that I was handing on to him—a good friend—a fundamentally lousy job. A job whose enormous complexity was only really appreciated by your immediate staff, who see the office working on a daily basis. A job in which, no matter what good things you do for people, you will rarely hear a "thank you." A job in which you are constantly translating budgetary and managerial concerns of central administration to a faculty concerned almost exclusively with its own teaching and research priorities—and vice versa. A job in which everyone and every constituency want you to serve *their* interests, as though there were no others. (Kolodny 1998, 27)

> Amid the daily swirl of unpleasant personnel problems, shortfalls in equipment budgets, inability to offer a competitive salary to a prized recruit, wars over the space allocation, lengthy and inane requests from cen-

tral administration for seemingly irrelevant data—amid all these problems that drive deans into rage or despondency or both, fantasy sometimes takes over. (Tucker and Bryan 1991, 1)

> In many cases, chairpersons receive extra compensation and other perquisites, such as full-time summer appointments and more luxurious office space. The material and psychological rewards of the position are intended to compensate for frustrations encountered in the job, such as abrasive incidents with both deans and faculty members, longer hours, and reduced time for teaching and research. (Tucker 1992, 27)

As far back as 1949 (and probably further), administrators have been writing about their disgruntled, frustrating experiences. In his 1949 essay, "Dear Dean Misanthrope: Imaginary Correspondence on Educational Administration," Eldon Johnson expresses through fantasy-letters his exasperation with deaning. The essay begins with a dean's letter of resignation to "Dean Misanthrope": "I think you know that one of my reasons for recently surrendering the deanship and thus depriving myself of many pleasant associations with you and the other deans in the official administrative family was my profound dissatisfaction with the life of mutual suspicion and recrimination which faculty and administration always insist upon as the normal state of university affairs" (E. Johnson 1949/1968, 173). Dean Misanthrope responds: "As your recent resignation in effect confesses, this deaning business is no milk-and-water affair. You either do it or you don't do it. Those of us who survive don't let faculty relations eat our souls out and we don't get sentimental about democratizing administration" (ibid., 174). The caricature of the soulless dean whose only concern is the bottom line is even more forcefully expressed in John Ciardi's 1962 essay, "Deans—In a Manner of Speaking," written after resigning his post as a university professor. He channels his hostility at deans who, in his mind, have taken the business of education away from those who are most qualified to do it—professors. His vision of academia's future is that of a horrifyingly efficient and prosperous business enterprise (sound familiar?): "the final debauchery of our educational system [will amount to] [...] a diploma mill in which the mere matter of ideas is relegated to faculty clerks, while the decisions are made by chart-riding administrative brass in the golden swivel chairs" (1962/1968, 191). As suggested by these examples, a history of disappointment in academic administration might show us the collective emotional experiences of administrators over time. Such an analysis could have a number of uses: for example, it could become the basis for positing new administrative structures (as demonstrated by Kolodny 1998); describing and responding to the widespread culture of disappointment in academia; developing a wider frame of reference for WPA work and its connection to a conflicted history of academic administration; and analyzing the relationship between emotion and work in order to discern the effects on our sense of efficacy and willingness to posit change.

2. *We need to describe more fully the affective dimensions of our work through materialist analysis.* Some recent analyses of work in composition studies offer strategies for rethinking graduate training, professional development, and academic labor practices. Such analyses have largely sought to describe and, through materialist analysis, re-describe our work so as to generate productive change. For example, in *Terms of Work for Composition* Bruce Horner (2000) argues that we can best professionalize our work by viewing it as material social practice, as a historically located activity intertwined with socioeconomic development. Among other things, this view conceives student writing as a form of work *and* a form of working through the material conditions of the writing classroom. The result, Horner explains, is that student writing may come to be viewed as productive rather than commodified labor, as meaningful work that has value rather than as a perfunctory exchange between student and teacher. By continuing to view student writing as somehow not real, we imply that "work" refers exclusively to scholarship and decidedly not to teaching and/or student writing.

Other analyses of working conditions in composition studies suggest new models for professionalizing workers in the field. Two essays in *College Composition and Communication* underscore the need to devise pragmatic approaches to improving working conditions in composition. Michael Murphy, in "New Faculty for a New University" (2000), argues that we need to professionalize faculty as thoroughly as possible while recognizing that composition will never be able to escape its primary identification as a teaching discipline. He addresses the persistent problem of exploited part-time faculty by arguing for the creation of "professionalized career-track instructorships" (Murphy 2000, 25). Along similar lines, in "Meet the New Boss, Same as the Old Boss" (2000), Joseph Harris calls for "a new sort of class consciousness in composition, one that joins the interests of bosses and workers around the issue of good teaching for fair pay" (Harris 2000, 45). This class consciousness would emerge from a collective commitment to equitable compensation for good teaching. Murphy and Harris advocate alternatives to tenure that would provide job security; both identify non-tenure-track instructorships as one such alternative. Also, both identify reform—rather than radical institutional change—as the most expedient route to improving working conditions.

Absent from these analyses is the extent to which our work practices are embedded in a social framework composed of not only economic and professional issues, but also emotional ones. Because emotions express valuations of a community, descriptions of how we work must address the way in which emotion structures our professional activities. Emotion is a central component in social relations and is intertwined with issues of power and status in the work world. Like Marxist critics, I hold that labor is a process that produces *people* and, as such, it produces emotional dispositions that are compatible with specific workforce locations. If we are to posit good work practices, as Murphy and Harris seek to do, we need to address the ways in which our profession produces emotional dispositions for its workers. Such recognition would show that a significant component of working conditions is tied up with how economic, cultural, and political institutions nurture, stunt, and/or amplify certain emotional habits.

Alison Jaggar has argued convincingly that emotion and knowledge are mutually enabling: "There is a continuous feedback loop between our emotional constitution and our theorizing such that each continually modifies the other and is in principle inseparable from it" (Jaggar 1989, 147). Jaggar contends that as our emotional relations to the world change, we gain new insights and ways of conceptualizing the world (ibid., 148). It would follow, then, that when we develop a more sustained understanding of the emotional contexts of our work worlds, these responses will stimulate new insights, new visions of possibility, as well as different ways of seeing the work we do. Teaching and administration, for instance, need to be recognized as forms of intellectual *and* emotional labor that shape and are shaped by institutional attitudes toward students, scholarship, administrative work, collegiality, and so forth. Part of an institutional or departmental tone develops from its members' affective relations to their work. This tone, in turn, communicates a sense of what is possible, thinkable, and unthinkable. If tone may be said to reveal something about the emotional life of a department, then an important task before us is to identify and delineate the factors that lead communities of teachers and scholars to develop fossilized thinking or a loss of faith in other people and in the profession as a whole.

3. *We need to educate ourselves about how work is organized in the university and to provide administrative mentoring and professional development to graduate students and junior faculty.* As I have shown throughout

this chapter, emotion—specifically disappointment—functions as a site of control and repression within the academy. Yet emotion can also be galvanized to challenge and resist the "privatization and pathologizing of emotions" (Boler 1999, xiv). The disenfranchisement of WPAs occurs through a variety of different processes, one of which is surely the process of learning disappointment. If, however, we can show that disappointment is not sufficiently explained as private and pathological, then we can begin to think critically about disappointment as a very public ingredient in the political disenfranchisement of WPAs. Again, here I think WPAs can learn from administrative scholarship. Kolodny's book in particular is an excellent example of how to use disappointment as a basis for formulating change. For one thing, she insists that educating faculty about the way an institution is organized will establish a working relationship between faculty and "administrators, university development officers, and governing boards to secure the funding needed to sustain quality education into the next century" (Kolodny 1998, 14). Consistent with the goals of feminist WPAs, Kolodny posits a model of collaborative academic administration that seeks to involve in the decision-making process those very people—faculty, staff, administration, and students—who will be affected by the outcome. As she explains, these constituencies would "work together as true partners, sharing information and negotiating priorities" (ibid., 30). Kolodny goes on to offer a redefinition of leadership as "an inclusive collaborative activity because everyone would fully understand—and shoulder—the consequences of any decision and its alternatives" (ibid., 30; also see 16). Mentoring future administrators—and perhaps future faculty in general—should include instruction about institutional structures, values, and decision-making. Because education is constantly vulnerable to massive budget cuts and downsizing—while at the same time the darling of campaigning politicians—it seems to me vital that faculty members receive some education about how an institution works. These machinations directly affect our livelihood and our ability to provide quality education to students. They also teach us how decisions are made—crucial knowledge if we are to collectively organize for political change. Faculty need to know the proper channels through which to voice their perspectives.

In addition, teacher-training courses as well as courses dealing explicitly with WPA work present opportunities for discussing the relationship between emotion and academic work. Given that a great number of recent job openings in composition studies require WPA work, faculty have an ethical responsibility to make visible the pleasures and rewards as well as the frustrations and disappointments that such work entails. Passing on content knowledge and practical know-how should be complemented by frank discussions about working conditions and the affective landscape of professional life. This imperative, coupled with my focus on disappointment, runs the risk of painting a dismal picture of WPA work, one that may make current WPAs angry and/or uncomfortable. After all, the exceptional rewards of working with new teachers and new students—including the dynamic intellectual culture that develops from these relationships—is not fully acknowledged here. Yet I would argue that it is precisely the intellectual and emotional fulfillment of WPA work that makes the disappointments and frustrations especially bitter components of our work. These components certainly do not *define* WPA work, but they do help us to see the institutional nature of disappointment in academic work practices. Disappointment erects obstacles to the hopefulness that I believe is necessary to sustain teachers and learners. In fact, I would argue that teaching, at its foundation, is a hopeful enterprise: it requires belief in the possibility of those contested terms—literacy, community, and education—to shape people's lives in positive and productive ways. Hope is an emotional investment that we develop collaboratively; it is an act of mutuality that is nourished by our collective expectations as professionals in a larger community and as faculty members in local contexts. Teaching, learning, and administration are not simply intellectual activities that one masters, but a complex blend of emotional and professional issues that involve the whole person. Enroute to hope, can we speak candidly about professional inequities and disappointments without being regarded as doomsayers, as spoilers of the democratic identity that composition studies has constructed of itself?

Interchapter:
Experience and Emotion

> *How are we to negotiate the gap between the conservative fiction of*
> *experience as the ground of all truth-knowledge and the immense*
> *power of this fiction to enable and encourage student participation?*
> Diana Fuss, *Essentially Speaking*

After the initial publication of "More Than a Feeling" in *College English* (Micciche 2002), a discussion strand about the essay developed on WPA-L. In the course of this public discussion, *experience* emerged for some as an authorizing discourse determining whether people identified with what I named a "climate of disappointment" in the context of WPA. This seems only natural, given that experience very often forms the basis by which we gauge the relevance and assess the validity of an argument. Additionally, as Diana Fuss (1989) suggests in the preceding epigraph, experience as a basis for knowledge claims is both a fiction and a powerful, enabling resource. The enabling power is clear in WPA-L participants' efforts to understand disappointment within the framework of their own experiences. In the process, their experiential narratives illuminate the extent to which experience becomes intertwined with emotion:

I've been a WPA for (gasp) 21 years now. I've gone through ugly tenure battles twice at two different institutions and endured endless "here's why this idea won't work" meetings. And yet. To paraphrase Rick Bragg, I wouldn't trade my job for a gold monkey. Maybe being reared as an administrator (I ran the writing center at my grad school as a grad student) and assuming that that was what comp people back then did—administration was where the jobs were—set me up; maybe I enjoy the problem-solving, the occasional illusions of power (but not too much), and the infinite variety of being a WPA, never knowing what the day will bring. Maybe I've been lucky to have worked under three wonderful, supportive, rational chairs and supportive deans and, for more than a decade, in a department mercifully short on tensions that values, really values, good teaching. Maybe I'm awash in false consciousness and don't understand my situation. But I like what I do and keep my heels polished, for just those moments when I need to click them together three times. (Bullock 2002)

At the same time [as state budget cuts threaten my university's operations], we still have to provide writing classes for about 6,500 students each semester, and I have 150+ great teachers I get to work with, and an English Department that's supportive, in an overall healthy and vibrant large university, and so I don't share the "disappointment" that Laura writes about. (Glau 2002)

I don't think [the experience of disappointment] has much to do with age. I've been administering writing programs (first, a composition program within a traditional English department and later, an independent writing program) for the past eight years and haven't experienced the climate of disappointment that Laura describes.

That's not to say I haven't confronted moments of frustration typical to our work as WPAs. But I've enjoyed unimaginable opportunities to build a first-year curriculum, as well as an undergraduate minor in writing; to assemble a substantial group of specialists in Rhetoric and Composition (nearly all in tenure-track or tenured positions); to design assessment measures with real integrity; and the list goes on.

I'll be the first to admit that doing such large-scale, far-reaching work in just eight years has been exhausting. But I can honestly say that the work has been exhilarating. I never imagined I'd get to enjoy such a significant role in enhancing both the scope and the quality of writing instruction for students. (McDonald 2002)

In these postings each writer uses personal experience and history to offer a counter-narrative to my study of disappointment. Their reviews of working conditions interrupt my claims about affective dissonance and WPA largely by attributing their alternative experiences to vibrant and supportive working environments. In this way, emotional "truth" aligned with individual experience functions as a reliable basis from which to form judgments. These excerpts, like everyday encounters, illustrate that experience and emotion are in metonymic relation to one another, and as a result, experience attains and embodies unacknowledged emotional truths. For instance, in the excerpts above, the formative histories relayed by Bullock and McDonald and the healthy, supportive context described by Glau convey an emotioned investment in representing their work lives in positive terms. Their messages seem motivated by more than a desire to represent experience; they also emerge from a desire to link experience and emotion differently, to offer alternative constructions of the affective world of WPAing as they've encountered it and grown attached to and invested in it. Their experience *is* emotioned, which is distinct from saying that they speak about their experiences in emotional terms. And because experience is emotioned in everyday contexts, and emotions are generally thought of as natural and unmediated in such contexts, experience, too, takes on the status of the uncontestable and natural—that is, a status that transcends analysis.

Emotion and experience work together, then, to authenticate a particular view of things rooted in the personal realm. As Fuss writes, "'Experience' emerges as the essential truth of the individual subject, and personal 'identity' metamorphoses into knowledge" (Fuss 1989, 113). Although this seems foreseeable, especially in the context of an informal listserv discussion where narrativizing is central to how people communicate, this use of experience as a means for authenticating the affective domain presents some difficult questions regarding the potential for emotion to count in our scholarship. How emotion and experience get bound together, making experience a form of emotional testimony, is what interests me in looking back on the WPA-L discussion, for it presents an opportunity to think about the risks posed by making emotion an explicit term of study in classrooms, where experience, perceived as an emotional truth, threatens to negate critical thought by devolving into competing narratives that speak primarily to and about the self (which, I do not claim to be the case with the WPA-L discussion; rather, that discussion reads to me now like a heuristic for thinking through a familiar classroom occurrence). The use of experience as an authenticating discourse that validates emotional "truth" presents serious obstacles to positing emotion as a category of analysis, raising questions concerning how scholars and writing teachers can depict emotioned experience as a site of contestation and productive tension that generates usable insights to composition studies. How can we frame experience and emotion as tools for opening rather than closing interpretations?

Although the exercises described in Chapter Three, which draw from models of performativity, partly address strategies for using emotion as an inventional, generative source for critical thought, I realize that this set of practices is far from comprehensive. The need to further investigate this subject is obvious, especially because students in my classes tend to rely on experience, and their emotioned relation to it, as a way of authenticating a position, which is usually more individually "true" and verifiable than collectively so. Following from this use of emotion and experience, classroom discussions can include awkward silences and, beyond that, a hierarchy of competing experience-based narratives designed to critique or complicate some other student's experience as a not-so-credible last word—neither effect of which is inherently "bad." I would much prefer to see my students more consistently using emotioned experience to ask questions, develop analysis or critique, or generate openings to a given topic.

An example will make the point more clearly. In my undergraduate class on eating disorders, one student repeatedly claimed during discussions that women are worse off in contemporary culture than they were before the women's movement of the last century. Prior to the movement, women had less reason to worry about their bodies; with liberties come neuroses and pathological behaviors, she argued. The centerpiece of her position was her grandmother's life-experiences in the 1930s and 1940s. Her grandmother lived a traditional life as a homemaker, wife, and mother; she remained content with her role and position in the home and the culture, never seeking a job outside the home or the same rights as men. As a result, she led a happy life, unfettered by the self-obsessed behavior of women after the women's movement (among whom this student included herself and her classmates) who constantly critiqued their own and each other's bodies in an effort to compete in the marketplace, where looking great is very much a part of career success.

There was some agreement among class members regarding this student's theory about the women's movement, but there was also a general resistance to attributing women's eating issues to a single cause. Simultaneously, students sought to destabilize the women's movement theory, based on one grandmother's experiences, by producing numerous articulations of other grandmothers' experiences (which included, among other things, bouts of depression, alcoholism, addiction to sleeping pills, and so on), creating a cacophony of experiential dramas without much analysis or critical attentiveness to the issues. Before I knew it or had the wherewithal to shift our discussion to acknowledgment of the multicausation models that we had studied, we were adrift in a blur of experiential narratives, all of which were presented by students with some emotional attachment, as if each were bearing the real truth about our collective grandmothers. What transpired in the discussion was a perfect example of Fuss' claim that, in the classroom setting, "identities can often seem more rigidified, politics more personalized, and past histories more intensified" (Fuss 1989, 115).

What I needed was a way to interrogate experience, to introduce the idea that claims based on anecdotal experience can prevent us from grappling with the systemic nature of women's experiences. Even as they seek to make connections across differences, such claims can instead produce individualized accounts that fail to make meaningful connections. In "Reading and Writing Differences" Min-Zhan Lu (1998/2003) offers some direction on this point when she advocates writing assignments that highlight emotional distress as a tool for rethinking self and experience in order to help students grasp the physicality of oppression in people's lives. Lu sees the concept of experience as central to the emotion work of pedagogy. Critically studying experience, she contends, should "motivate us to care about another's differences and should disrupt the material conditions that have given rise to [that experience]" (Lu 1998/2003, 436), which contrasts with a use that allows the personal to elide differences. Lu's pedagogical strategy aims to produce emotional subjects who are conscious of others' pain and mistreatment and to create awareness of their own complicity in that pain and mistreatment.

Lu's interrogation of experience makes possible a more critical approach to how experience functions in classroom contexts. In order to extend this effort to account for emotion as a social discourse that adheres to judgments, beliefs, and values, as well as to narratives of experience, we need to position emotion as more than a tool that illuminates the materiality of experience. We need a strategy for addressing the interconnections between emotion and experience, because the turn to experience as a means of persuasion is inseparable from the emotional stickiness that shapes interpretations of reality. As the excerpts from the WPA-L indicate, telling one's story is a way of revealing emotioned commitments to how and what we value. It is also a way of using experience to generate affective value that sticks to a particular story or rendering of reality. In short, positioning experience as a site of critique and interrogation does not go far enough because what remains is the tangled relationship between emotion and experience that motivates our use of experience as evidence in the first place. We need what Fuss calls a "double gesture," by which she means an effort "both to theorize essentialist spaces from which to speak and, simultaneously, to deconstruct these spaces to keep them from solidifying. Such a double gesture involves...the responsibility to historicize, to examine each deployment of essence, each appeal to experience, each claim to identity in the complicated contextual frame in which it is made" (ibid., 118).

Thus, our next challenge is to learn how to address claims to experience and emotion in student discussion and in our own writing. Rendering emotion in more explicitly rhetorical terms by foregrounding what emotions *do* represents one small move toward destabilizing the *essence* of feeling and experience without denying the power and value of both. The purpose of doing so lies in the potential to generate a more critical understanding of how we draw on available resources—here, experience and emotion—in order to persuade and demonstrate, to make better use of words, images, and all manner of signs. Denaturalizing emotion and experience with our students might enable them to use these resources more adeptly in the creation of discourse, a central goal of our courses.

Conclusion:
Emotion Matters

Emotion matters are difficult, dense, subjective, personal, communal, socially lived and understood, historical and cultural, impossible to avoid, intertwined with all that we say, think, write, know, withhold, remember, and wish to forget. Emotion matters drive motives for action, speech, judgment, and decision-making. Emotion matters have materiality because they are lived and expressed in and through bodies and cultures.

Emotion forms part of how we come to develop attachments to others as well as to objects and ideas. Emotion matters to teachers because the classroom is alive with bodies, hearts, and selves, and because learning is joyous, exciting, frightening, risky, passionate, boring, disappointing, and enraging. Emotion matters are inscribed in the teaching situation, a point too often forgotten. The history of education provides numerous glimpses of links among emotion, learning, and teaching. Colonial education, for example, sought to create social stability through the teaching of Protestant religious beliefs, placing faith, a way of feeling about God and country, at the cornerstone of a proper education. Following the American Revolution, education cultivated nationalism through a shared language and culture, generating a patriotic unification among citizens characterized by an emotional attachment to the exercise of freedom and individualism. Early nineteenth-century education embraced the idea that moral character—including politeness, cleanliness, and respect for others—could be created through the organized institutional environment that schooling provided. Schooling moral character amounted to socializing students for the world, a process that inevitably involves training in emotional display and expression appropriate for "civilized" society.

In the late nineteenth century, as industrialism gained strength in the American economy, education aimed to create citizens who could contribute to economic growth. The dominant emotional constitution desired in students during this period was fierce competitiveness and patriotism, both expressions of the gains of a newly formed industrial capitalism. This mission can be contrasted with John Dewey's efforts in the early 1900s to describe education as a means for bringing people together and for modeling an idea of community strengthened by differences.

Emotion matters to *writing* teachers, who remain indebted to Dewey's belief in the democratizing function of education, because writing is mediated by language, bodies, and culture; writing involves sticky attachments that evolve and materialize through the writing process, including emotioned attachments that find their way onto the page sometimes against our will or without our conscious assent. Donna Haraway describes this as "the experience of working through a sentence and finding that it's committed me to half a dozen positions that I don't hold, literally because of the material density of language" (qtd. in Olson 1996, 4). Writing, she says, "is itself a material process of thinking . . . there's no thinking process outside of some materiality" (ibid.). And I would add, there's no such thing as emotion outside embodied thought and experience, another way of naming materiality.

Emotion expression and reception, too, are material processes—they take form in speech, image, body, and action. Thus, emotions are embedded in rhetorical activity and so also inform overarching ideas about how best to teach the arts of rhetoric, including writing. In composition studies, teaching methods and the very act of teaching pulsate with optimism. Concern about conditions that threaten to dampen the affirming spirit of teaching surfaces throughout composition scholarship. For example, Hephzibah Roskelly and Kate Ronald propose that romanticism and pragmatism can fend against cynicism, an affective stance that leads to a "pedagogical and scholarly crisis of the spirit, a poverty of belief more damaging to the cause of real literacy than economic deprivation" (Roskelly and Ronald 1998, 2). They hope to give people "a reason to believe in the vocation of teaching and its uses in the world" (ibid., 27).

Positioning teaching as an activity that is made possible by belief, passion, spirit, and hope may seem like grand talk, but this has never stopped teachers from describing their work as a *calling*, a utopian drive to recognize and energize students' untapped potentialities. Victor Villanueva, in his memoir *Bootstraps*, describes classrooms as "ideal site[s] in which to affect change; the classroom, where we come in contact with so many, the many who in turn will come in contact with many more. It's a utopian hope, but it is the utopian possibility that makes for a teacher" (1993, 121).

Hope and belief constitute the sticky adhesive that binds together the majority of contemporary teaching practices. Investment in producing compassionate citizens through liberatory pedagogies, as a result of which people care for and about others, is made possible by desire for change and belief in teaching as a proper, even necessary, venue through which to facilitate it. This is different from projecting certain emotions onto student bodies, as early versions of critical pedagogy have been critiqued for doing, because more recent teaching methods are invested in what Ahmed calls wonder, which involves "learning to see the world as something that does not have to be, and as something that came to be, over time, and with work" (Ahmed 2004, 180). In this sense, specific emotions are not the desired outcome of teaching—as one might argue was the case for critical pedagogies that valorized righteous anger—but emerge from the process of teaching toward possibilities and openings of all sorts.

Amy Winans demonstrates this kind of commitment in "Local Pedagogies and Race" (2005). To foreground and question whiteness as signifying a learned affect about self and other, Winans begins from what students already know and feel about race. She describes her efforts to develop a localized pedagogy of race and especially whiteness at her predominantly white university, Susquehanna University, in rural Pennsylvania. Rather than assume that students are operating under the illusion of false consciousness about racial differences and injustices, she seeks to acknowledge the embodied experiences that have influenced her students' thinking (and absence of thinking) about race. She calls this "taking students' ethical beliefs and goals seriously rather than seeing them as misguided assumptions to be worked through," even as she teaches students who regularly assume "that the only people who have a racial identity and who are affected by race are people of color" (Winans 2005, 263, 254). Winans is careful to avoid an essentialized notion of whiteness, which is usually dependent on the construction of a "middle-class white student who needs to learn about his or her own racism" (ibid., 256), and instead hopes to recognize the different ways in which whiteness is lived. Among other things, this means that she does not equate whiteness with white people because as a group they benefit from ideologies of whiteness unevenly.

Her goal is to teach students how to "question their own narratives, the standpoints from which they craft those narratives, and the consequences of those narratives" (ibid., 258). Her students do their own emotion work as they grapple with the significance and origin of the positions they hold on race and whiteness. Winans is interested in creating classroom conditions through which students question and analyze the motives informing their views of race. By using writing and self-reflective analysis of writing as tools for recognizing and exploring students' "strong, often unstated emotions" (ibid., 263) about race and whiteness, Winans positions writing as a viable medium through which we may uncover the operations of whiteness. Moreover, she designates writing classrooms as appropriate sites for engaging in the political and emotional stickiness of whiteness. Winans wants her white students to think about their own performance of whiteness in ways that complicate notions of guilt and innocence because she hopes students will come to terms with the complexity of lived racial identity in our culture. I believe she takes this as her focus in order to instruct students in how to compose and revise feelings about self and other. In other words, she works with students to make visible the resonances of race normally submerged. Her pedagogy implicitly asks students to consider the relationship between emotions—in this case, guilt, shame, pride, fear, sadness, anger, and empathy—and whiteness as an often invisible racial category.

As this example suggests, once we learn to name the presence of emotion in pedagogical goals, administrative work, and intellectual commitments, we must also admit a language and a framework for understanding emotion as that which cannot be reduced to an appeal, a play on feelings, or a resource operating outside reason and meaning. Seeing emotion as a category of analysis and part of the adhesive that generates belief, attachment, and investment presents an opportunity to rethink instruction of rhetorical concepts. At a minimum, this rethinking should involve a reconsideration of emotion in relation to audience, ethos, and logos. Said differently, I think compositionists need to "go off the map" in order to think outside what is established and codified as representative models of teaching, learning, and conceptualizing rhetoric. As an alternative framework for doing intellectual work, one that courts wonder, I find environmental theorist Paul Wapner's call for practicing "wild mind" energizing and necessary for the creation of projects, like this one, intent on concept undoing and remaking. In "Ecological Thinking: Studying Global Environmental Politics with a Wild Mind and a Mindful Heart" (2003), he argues that those interested in studying and teaching the evolving field of global environmental politics must exercise a "wild mind." For him, this term

> denotes an intellectual *attitude* that is willing to address issues outside of established categories. It suggests a *way of seeing* the world that is marked by excitement and passion and by a *form of inquiry* that is courageous enough to proceed without reliable conceptual maps. Most of all, wild mind means a commitment to freeing our own intellect and exploring where our thoughts take us rather than worrying about replicating the ideas of others. (Wapner 2003, 20; my emphasis)

What's *wild* about wild mind is feeling compelled to wander into unknown territory without concern for what one may or may not find there. This wildness also involves freeing oneself of the anxiety involved in replication—saying what others have said, but differently. I think of how the first stage in my writing process is always replication in the form of summary; belabored and reverential, my summaries are boring and lifeless. Yet, they are my starting point, the place from which I strive for a more adventurous attitude toward my subject matter so that I may begin to see it differently, beyond the terms established by others.

Wild mind may not be entirely possible in practice—after all, what others have said and discovered *does* matter and *is* worrying—but I see it as an aspirational affect for doing scholarship and for teaching students something about the intellectual work entailed in writing, especially when teaching writing through strategies that have long occupied subordinate spaces. Wild mind epitomizes to me the idea that emotion, and the application of emotion as a rhetorical and critical term, opens possibilities and generates different orientations to others as well as to objects; this construction contrasts with the potential for emotions to create stasis when functioning as the adhesive by which people become so invested in a belief that contradictions and contrary facts fail to shift it. The idea of emotion, as that which opens or closes, is nudged into rhetorical domains by questions focused on what emotion *does* rather than what it *is* or where we see it being *used*. Emotion as performative emphasizes the *does*, making clear that, as teachers, we cannot install empathy over indifference or political anger over contentment among our students, for emotion does not belong to people but is produced among them.

To situate emotion in the realm of rhetoric requires teachers and students to abandon common sense and "natural" thinking, neither of which allows us to detach emotion from individuals or from the category of "the personal." This is not to say that people do not feel emotions, do not experience them personally. It means that emotions are without singular origins. They are produced among people, through interaction, in contexts where the swirl of affective meanings is variable rather transhistorical and transcultural. Introducing this idea in the classroom and in disciplinary scholarship is an exercise in wild mind because there is no reliable conceptual map to guide us and no sustained voice to replicate. At stake in crafting rhetorics of emotion that go beyond traditional applications of the emotional appeal is what Ahmed describes as "the 'truths' of this world," which are "dependent on emotions, on how they move subjects, and stick them together" (Ahmed 2004,

170). That is, those things that operate as "truths" in the "world" of composition studies—i.e., students can be empowered through teaching practices, or writers have an authentic voice—are more than guiding principles that have long been staple components of writing instruction. Following Ahmed's thinking, these truths are beholden to emotional attachments to a certain way of seeing our work, our students, and ourselves. I believe that exploring what is embedded in these attachments promises to unearth a new set of questions among composition scholars that is certain to expand the reach of rhetorics of emotion.

Works Cited

Abu-Lughod, Lila, and Catherine A. Lutz. 1990. "Introduction: Emotion, Discourse, and the Politics of Everyday Life." In *Language and the Politics of Emotion*, edited by Lutz and Abu-Lughod, 1–23. Cambridge, UK: Cambridge University Press.

Ahmed, Sara. 2004. *The Cultural Politics of Emotion*. New York: Routledge.

Alexander, Jonathan, and William P. Banks. 2004. "Sexualities, Technologies, and the Teaching of Writing: A Critical Overview." *Computers and Composition* 21:273–93.

Alexander, Jonathan, and Michelle Gibson, eds. 2004. "Queer Theory." Special issue, *JAC* 24:1–111.

Aristotle. 1991. *On Rhetoric: A Theory of Civic Discourse*. Translated by George A. Kennedy. New York: Oxford University Press.

Baldwin, James. [1955] 2002. Excerpt from *Notes of a Native Son*. In *Ways of Reading: An Anthology for Writers*, 6th ed., edited by David Bartholomae and Anthony Petrosky, 49–68. Boston: Bedford/St. Martin's.

Barr-Ebest, Sally. 1995. "Gender Differences in Writing Program Administration." *WPA: Writing Program Administration* 18 (Spring):53–73.

Barrett, Lisa Feldman. 2005. "Feeling Is Perceiving: Core Affect and Conceptualization in the Experience of Emotion." In *Emotion and Consciousness*, edited by Barrett et al., 255–84. New York: Guilford Press.

———, Paula M. Niedenthal, and Piotr Winkielman, eds. 2005. *Emotion and Consciousness*. New York: Guilford Press.

Bartholomae, David, and Anthony Petrosky. 2002. *Ways of Reading: An Anthology for Writers*, 6th ed. Boston: Bedford/St. Martin's.

Bartky, Sandra Lee. 1990. "Feeding Egos and Tending Wounds: Deference and Disaffection in Women's Emotional Labor." In *Femininity and Domination: Studies in Phenomenology of Oppression*, 99–138. New York: Routledge.

Basalla, Susan, and Maggie Debelius. 2001. *"So What Are You Going to Do with That?": A Guide to Career-Changing for M.A.'s and PH.D.'s*. New York: Farrar, Straus and Giroux.

Beech, Jennifer, and Julie Lindquist. 2004. "The Work Before Us: Attending to English Departments' Poor Relations." *Pedagogy* 4.2:171–89.

Belenky, Mary Field, Blythe McVicker Clinchy, Nancy Rule Goldberger, and Jill Mattuck Tarule. 1986. *Women's Ways of Knowing: The Development of Self, Voice, and Mind.* New York: Basic Books.

Berlant, Lauren. 2000. "The Subject of True Feeling: Pain, Privacy, and Politics." In *Transformations: Thinking through Feminism*, edited by Sara Ahmed, Jane Kilby, Celia Lury, Maureen McNeil, and Beverley Skeggs, 33–47. New York: Routledge.

Berlin, James A. 1987. *Rhetoric and Reality: Writing Instruction in American Colleges, 1900–1985.* Carbondale, IL: SIUP.

Berndt, Michael, and Amy Muse. 2004. *Composing a Civic Life: A Rhetoric and Readings for Inquiry and Action.* New York: Pearson Longman.

Bérubé, Michael. 1998. *The Employment of English: Theory, Jobs and the Future of Literary Studies.* New York: New York University Press.

Bizzell, Patricia, and Bruce Herzberg. 2001. *The Rhetorical Tradition: Readings from Classical Times to the Present*, 2d ed. Boston: Bedford/St. Martin's.

Bloom, Lynn Z. 1992. "I Want a Writing Director." *College Composition and Communication* 43:176–78.

Boler, Megan. 1999. *Feeling Power: Emotions and Education.* New York: Routledge.

Bordo, Susan. 1990. "Feminism, Postmodernism, and Gender-Scepticism." In *Feminism/Postmodernism*, edited by Nicholson, 133–56. New York: Routledge.

Bourdieu, Pierre. 1992. *The Logic of Practice.* Stanford, CA: Stanford University Press.

Bouson, J. Brooks. 2005. "True Confessions: Uncovering the Hidden Culture of Shame in English Studies." *JAC* 25.4:625–50.

Bousquet, Marc, Tony Scott, and Leo Parascondola, eds. 2004. *Tenured Bosses and Disposable Teachers: Writing Instruction in the Managed University.* Carbondale, IL: SIUP.

Bowles, Samuel, and Herbert Gintis. 1976. *Schooling in Capitalist America: Educational Reform and the Contradictions of Economic Life.* New York: Basic Books.

Bramblett, Anne, and Alison Knoblauch, eds. 2002. *What to Expect When You're Expected to Teach: The Anxious Craft of Teaching Composition.* Portsmouth, NH: Boynton/Cook.

Brennan, Teresa. 2004. *The Transmission of Affect.* Ithaca, NY: Cornell University Press.

Brody, Miriam. 1993. *Manly Writing: Gender, Rhetoric, and the Rise of Composition.* Carbondale, IL: SIUP.

Brown, Wendy. 1995. *States of Injury: Power and Freedom in Late Modernity.* Princeton, NJ: Princeton University Press.

Brumberg, Joan Jacobs. [1988] 2000. *Fasting Girls: The History of Anorexia Nervosa.* New York: Vintage.

Bullock, Richard. 2002. "Re: Disappointment and WPA Work." *Writing Program Administrators Listserv.* WPA-L@asu.edu (7 Mar 2002) <http://lists.asu.edu/cgi-bin/wa?A2=ind0203&L=wpa-l&D=1&O=D&F=&S=&P=12190.>

———, and John Trimbur, eds. 1991. *The Politics of Writing Instruction: Postsecondary.* Portsmouth, NH: Boynton/Cook.

Bush, George W. "President Calls for Constitutional Amendment Protecting Marriage." 2006. *The White House: President George W. Bush.* 24 February 2004. 12 June 2006. www.whitehouse.gov/news/releases/2004/02/20040224-2.html.

Campbell, Kermit E. 2005. *"Getting' Our Groove On": Rhetoric Language, and Literacy for the Hip Hop Generation.* Detroit, MI: Wayne State University Press.

Ciardi, John. [1962] 1968. "Deans—In a Manner of Speaking." In *The Academic Deanship in American Colleges and Universities,* edited by Dibden, 184–191. Carbondale, IL: SIUP

Clark, Suzanne. 1994. "Rhetoric, Social Construction, and Gender: Is It Bad to Be Sentimental?" In *Writing Theory and Critical Theory,* edited by John Clifford and John Schilb, 96–108. New York: MLA.

Connors, Robert J. 1990. "Overwork/Underpay: Labor and Status of Composition Teachers Since 1880." *Rhetoric Review* 9.1 (Fall):108–25.

———. 1991. "Rhetoric in the Modern University: The Creation of an Underclass." In *The Politics of Writing Instruction,* edited by Bullock and Trimbur, 55–84. Portsmouth, NH: Boynton/Cook.

Conquergood, Dwight. 1995. "Of Caravans and Carnivals: Performance Studies in Motion." *The Drama Review* 39.4:137–41.

———. 2002. "Performance Studies: Interventions and Radical Research." *The Drama Review* 46.2:145–56.

Corbett, Edward P. J., and Robert J. Connors. 1999. *Classical Rhetoric for the Modern Student,* 4th ed. New York: Oxford University Press.

Covino, William A. 1988. *The Art of Wondering: A Revisionist Return to the History of Rhetoric.* Portsmouth, NH: Boynton/Cook.

Craib, Ian. 1994. *The Importance of Disappointment.* New York: Routledge.

Crowley, Sharon. 1998. *Composition in the University: Historical and Polemical Essays.* Pittsburgh, PA: University of Pittsburgh Press.
———, and Debra Hawhee. 1999. *Ancient Rhetorics for Contemporary Students,* 2d ed. Boston: Allyn and Bacon.

Cvetovich, Ann. 2003. *An Archive of Feelings: Trauma, Sexuality, and Lesbian Public Cultures.* Durham, NC: Duke University Press.

Davis, D. Diane. 2000. *Breaking Up [at] Totality: A Rhetoric of Laughter.* Carbondale, IL: SIUP.

Deans, Thomas. 2000. *Writing Partnerships: Service-Learning in Composition.* Urbana, IL: NCTE.

Diamond, Elin, ed. 1996. *Performance and Cultural Politics.* New York: Routledge.

Dibden, Arthur J., ed. 1968. *The Academic Deanship in American Colleges and Universities.* Carbondale, IL: SIUP.

Dickson, Marcia. 1993. "Directing Without Power: Adventures in Constructing a Model of Feminist Writing Programs Administration." In *Writing Ourselves Into the Story,* edited by Fontaine and Hunter, 140–153. Carbondale, IL: SIUP.

Dixon, Kathleen, ed. 1998. *Outbursts in Academe: Multiculturalism and Other Sources of Conflict.* Portsmouth, NH: Heinemann.

Durst, Russel. 1999. *Collision Course: Conflict, Negotiation, and Learning in College Composition.* Urbana, IL: NCTE.

Edbauer, Jennifer H. 2005. "(Meta)Physical Graffiti: 'Getting Up' as Affective Writing Model." *JAC* 25.1:131–59.

Ede, Lisa. 2004. *Situating Composition: Composition Studies and the Politics of Location.* Carbondale, IL: SIUP.

Enos, Theresa. 1996. *Gender Roles and Faculty Lives in Rhetoric and Composition.* Carbondale, IL: SIUP.

Faigley, Lester. 1993. *Fragments of Rationality: Postmodernity and the Subject of Composition.* Pittsburgh, PA: University of Pittsburgh Press.

Ferguson, Ann. 1991. *Sexual Democracy, Women, Oppression and Revolution.* Boulder, CO: Westview Press.

Fineman, Stephen, ed. 2000. *Emotion in Organizations,* 2d ed. London: Sage.

Fish, Stanley. 2000. "Nice Work If You Can Get Them to Do It." *ADE Bulletin* 126 (Fall):1–5. 24 May 2001 <http://www.ade.org/ade/bulletin/n126/126015.htm>.

Fishman, Jenn, Andrea Lunsford, Beth McGregor, and Mark Otuteye. 2005. "Performing Writing, Performing Literacy." *College Composition and Communication* 57:224–52.

Fitts, Karen, and Alan W. France, eds. 1995. *Left Margins: Cultural Studies and Composition Pedagogy.* Albany, NY: SUNY.

Flax, Jane. 1990. "Postmodernism and Gender Relations in Feminist Theory." In *Feminism/Postmodernism*, by Nicholson, 39–62. New York: Routledge.

Flynn, Elizabeth A. 1995. "Review: Feminist Theories/Feminist Composition." *College English* 57:201–12.

Fontaine, Sheryl I., and Susan Hunter, eds. 1993. *Writing Ourselves into the Story: Unheard Voices from Composition Studies.* Carbondale, IL: SIUP.

Fuss, Diana. 1989. *Essentially Speaking: Feminism, Nature and Difference.* New York: Routledge.

Gale, Xin Liu, and Fredric G. Gale, eds. 1999. *(Re)Visioning Composition Textbooks: Conflicts of Culture, Ideology, and Pedagogy.* Albany, NY: SUNY.

Gallagher, Chris. 2005. "We Compositionists: Toward Engaged Professionalism." *JAC* 25.1:75–99.

Garry, Ann, and Marilyn Pearsall, eds. 1989. *Women, Knowledge, and Reality: Explorations in Feminist Philosophy.* Boston: Unwin Hyman.

George, Diana, ed. 1999. *Kitchen Cooks, Plate Twirlers, and Troubadours: Writing Program Administrators Tell Their Stories.* Portsmouth, NH: Boynton/Cook.

Gere, Anne Ruggles. 1994. "Kitchen Tables and Rented Rooms: The Extracurriculum of Composition." *College Composition and Communication* 45:75–92.

Gilman, Charlotte Perkins. [1892] 2001. "The Yellow Wallpaper." In *The Longman Anthology of Women's Literature*, edited by Mary K. DeShazer, 263–74. New York: Longman.

Gilyard, Keith. 1996. *Let's Flip the Script: An African American Discourse on Language, Literature and Learning.* Detroit, MI: Wayne State University Press.

Giroux, Henry, and Peter McLaren, eds. 1989. *Critical Pedagogy, the State, and Cultural Struggle.* Albany, NY: SUNY.

Glau, Gregory. 2002. "Re: Disappointment and WPA Work." *Writing Program Administrators Listserv.* WPA-L@asu.edu (7 Mar 2002). <http://lists.asu.edu/cgi-bin/wa?A2=ind0203&L=wpa-l&D=1 &O=D&F=&S=&P=21694>.

Goggin, Maureen Daly. 2000. *Authoring a Discipline: Scholarly Journals and the Post–World War II Emergence of Rhetoric and Composition.* Mahwah, NJ: Lawrence Erlbaum Associates.

Goodburn, Amy, and Carrie Shively Leverenz. 1998. "Feminist Writing Program Administration: Resisting the Bureaucrat Within." In *Feminism and Composition Studies: In Other Words*, edited by Jarratt and Worsham, 276–90. New York: MLA

Gore, Al. 2000. "In His Remarks, Gore Says He Will Help Bush 'Bring America Together.'" *New York Times* 14 Dec. 2000. 19 Dec. 2000 <http://nytimes.qpass.com/qpass-archives>.

Gottschalk, Katherine K. 2002. "Contact Zones: Composition's Content in the University." In *Professing in the Contact Zone: Bringing Theory and Practice Together,* edited by Janice M. Wolff, 58–78. Urbana, IL: NCTE.

Grant, Stephanie. 1995. *The Passion of Alice.* New York: Bantam.

Grimm, Nancy Barbara Conroy Maloney. 1999. "'The Way the Rich People Does It': Reflections on Writing Center Administration and the Search for Status." In *Kitchen Cooks, Plate Twirlers and Troubadours,* edited by George, 14–25. Portsmouth, NH: Boynton/Cook.

Gunner, Jeanne. 1994. "Decentering the WPA." *WPA: Writing Program Administration* 18.1–2:8–15.

———. 1997. "Politicizing the Portland Resolution." *WPA: Writing Program Administration* 20.3:23–30.

Haraway, Donna. 1990. "A Manifesto for Cyborgs: Science, Technology, and Socialist Feminism in the 1980s." In *Feminism/ Postmodernism,* by Nicholson, 190–233. New York: Routledge.

Hargreaves, Andy. 1994. *Changing Teachers, Changing Times: Teachers' Work and Culture in the Postmodern Age.* New York: Teachers College Press.

Harris, Joseph. 2000. "Meet the New Boss, Same as the Old Boss: Class Consciousness in Composition." *College Composition and Communication* 52:43–68.

Hawhee, Debra. 2004. *Bodily Arts: Rhetoric and Athletics in Ancient Greece.* Austin: University of Texas Press.

Herman, Peter C. 2000. *Day Late, Dollar Short: The Next Generation and the New Academy.* Albany, NY: SUNY Press.

Herrick, James A. 2001. *The History and Theory of Rhetoric: An Introduction,* 2d ed. Boston: Allyn and Bacon.

Hesford, Wendy S. 1998. "'Ye Are Witnesses': Pedagogy and the Politics of Identity." In *Feminism and Composition Studies,* edited by Jarratt and Worsham, 132–52. New York: MLA.

Hickey, Dona J. 1999. *Figures of Thought for College Writers.* Mountain View, CA: Mayfield Publishing.

Hochschild, Arlie Russell. 1983. *The Managed Heart: Commercialization of Human Feeling.* Berkeley: University of California Press.

Holbrook, Sue Ellen. 1991. "Women's Work: The Feminizing of Composition Studies." *Rhetoric Review* 9:201–29.

Holt, Mara. 1999. "On Coming to Voice." In *Kitchen Cooks, Plate Twirlers, and Troubadours,* edited by George, 26–43. Portsmouth, NH: Boynton/Cook.

Horner, Bruce. 2000. *Terms of Work for Composition: A Materialist Critique.* Albany, NY: SUNY.

Hult, Christine A. 1995. "The Scholarship of Administration." In *Resituating Writing,* edited by Janangelo and Hansen, 119–131. Portsmouth, NH: Boynton/Cook.

————, et al. 2001. "The Portland Resolution." 24 May 2001 <http://wpa.council.org>.

Jacobs, Dale. 2005. "What's Hope Got to Do with It?: Toward a Theory of Hope and Pedagogy." *JAC* 25.4:783–802.

————, and Laura R. Micciche, eds. 2003. *A Way to Move: Rhetorics of Emotion and Composition Studies.* Portsmouth, NH: Boynton/Cook.

Jaggar, Alison M. 1989. "Love and Knowledge: Emotion in Feminist Epistemology." In *Women, Knowledge, and Reality,* edited by Garry and Pearsall, 129–55. Boston: Unwin Hyman.

Janangelo, Joseph, and Kristine Hansen, eds. 1995. *Resituating Writing: Constructing and Administering Writing Programs.* Portsmouth, NH: Boynton/Cook.

Jarratt, Susan C. 1991. *Rereading the Sophists: Classical Rhetoric Refigured.* Carbondale, IL: SIUP.

————, and Lynn Worsham, eds. 1998. *Feminism and Composition Studies: In Other Words.* New York: MLA.

Johnson, Eldon L. [1949] 1968. "Dear Dean Misanthrope: Imaginary Correspondence on Educational Administration." In *The Academic Deanship in American Colleges and Universities,* edited by Dibden, 173–83. Carbondale, IL: SIUP

Johnson, Mark. 1999. "Embodied Reason." In *Perspectives on Embodiment: The Intersections of Nature and Culture,* edited by Gail Weiss and Honi Fern Haber, 81–102. New York: Routledge.

Jones, Joni L. 2002. "Teaching in the Borderlands." In *Teaching Performance Studies,* edited by Stucky and Wimmer, 175–90. Carbondale, IL: SIUP.

Kelchtermans, Geert. 1996. "Teacher Vulnerability: Understanding Its Moral and Political Roots." *Cambridge Journal of Education* 26:307–24.

Knoblauch, C.H., and Lil Brannon. 1993. *Critical Teaching and the Idea of Literacy.* Portsmouth, NH: Boynton/Cook.

Kolodny, Annette. 1998. *Failing the Future: A Dean Looks at Higher Education in the Twenty-first Century.* Durham, NC: Duke University Press.

Lakoff, George, and Mark Johnson. 1980. *Metaphors We Live By.* Chicago: University of Chicago Press.

Lamott, Anne. 1999. "Shitty First Drafts." In *Figures of Thought,* by Hickey. Mountain View, CA; Mayfield Publishing.

Levy, Matthew A. 2005. "Cynicism, Social Epistemic, and the Institutional Context of College Composition." *JAC* 25.2: 347–70.

Lindquist, Julie. 2004. "Class Affects, Classroom Affectations: Working Through the Paradoxes of Strategic Empathy." *College English* 67:187–209.

Logan, Shirley Wilson. 1995. *With Pen and Voice: A Critical Anthology of Nineteenth-Century African American Women.* Carbondale: SIUP.

———. 1998. "'When and Where I Enter': Race, Gender, and Composition Studies." In *Feminism and Composition Studies,* edited by Jarratt and Worsham, 45–57. New York: MLA

Lorde, Audre. 1984. "The Master's Tools Will Never Dismantle the Master's House." In *Sister Outsider: Essays and Speeches,* 110–13. Freedom, CA: The Crossing Press, 1984.

Lu, Min-Zhan. [1998] 2003. "Reading and Writing Differences: The Problematic of Experience." In *Feminism and Composition: A Critical Sourcebook,* edited by Gesa E. Kirsch et al., 436–46. Boston: Bedford/St. Martin's.

Lutz, Catherine A. 1990. "Engendered Emotion: Gender, Power, and the Rhetoric of Emotional Control in American Discourse." In *Language and the Politics of Emotion,* edited by Lutz and Abu-Lughod, 69–91. Cambridge, UK: Cambridge University Press.

———, and Lila Abu-Lughod, eds. 1990. *Language and the Politics of Emotion.* Cambridge, UK: Cambridge University Press.

Lynch, William F. [1965] 1974. *Images of Hope: Imagination as Healer of the Hopeless.* Notre Dame, IN: University of Notre Dame Press.

Madison, D. Soyini, and Judith Hamera. 2006a. "Performance Studies at the Intersections." In *The Sage Handbook of Performance Studies,* edited by Madison and Hamera, xi–xxv. London: Sage.

———, eds. 2006b. *The Sage Handbook of Performance Studies.* London: Sage.

Marcus, George E., W. Russell Neuman, and Michael Mackuen. 2000. *Affective Intelligence and Political Judgment.* Chicago: University of Chicago Press.

Marx, Karl. [1844] 1963. *The Economic and Philosophical Manuscripts,* edited by Dirk Struick. New York: International Publishers. (Original work published 1844)

McConnel, Frances Ruhlen. 1993. "Freeway Flyers: The Migrant Workers of the Academy." In *Writing Ourselves into the Story,* edited by Fontaine and Hunter, 40–58. Cambridge, IL: SIUP.

McCoy, Arielle. December 3, 2004. "Hearing a Whisper in a Room Full of Shouting." Department of English, University of Cincinnati.

McDonald, Christina. 2002. "Re: Disappointment and WPA Work." *Writing Program Administrators Listserv.* WPA-L@asu.edu (8 Mar 2002). <http://lists.asu.edu/cgi-bin/wa?A2=ind0203&L=wpa-l&D=1&O=D&F=&S=&P=19119>.

McLeod, Susan H. 1997. *Notes on the Heart: Affective Issues in the Writing Classroom.* Carbondale, IL: SIUP.

Meyerson, Debra E. 2000. "If Emotions Were Honoured: A Cultural Analysis." In *Emotion in Organizations*, edited by Fineman, 167–83. Cambridge, IL: SIUP.

Micciche, Laura R. 2002. "More Than a Feeling: Disappointment and WPA Work." *College English* 64:432–58.

Miller, Hildy. 1996. "Postmasculinist Directions in Writing Program Administration." *WPA: Writing Program Administration* 20.1–2: 49–61.

Miller, Richard. 1994. "Fault Lines in the Contact Zone." *College English* 56:389–408.

———. 1999. "Critique's the Easy Part: Choice and the Scale of Relative Oppression." In *Kitchen Cooks, Plate Twirlers, and Troubadours*, edited by George, 3–13. Portsmouth, NJ: Boynton/Cook.

Miller, Susan. 1991a. "The Feminization of Composition." In *The Politics of Writing Instruction*, edited by Bullock and Trimbur, 39–54. Portsmouth, NH: Boynton/Cook.

———. 1991b. *Textual Carnivals: The Politics of Composition.* Carbondale, IL: SIUP.

———. 2005. "The Evidence of Our Sensibilities." Rev. of *Liberating Voices: Writing at the Bryn Mawr Summer School for Women Workers*, by Karyn L. Hollis, and *Minor Re/Visions: Asian American Literacy Narratives as a Rhetoric of Citizenship*, by Morris Young. *College Composition and Communication* 56:688–700.

Moraga, Cherríe, and Gloria Anzaldúa, eds. 1981. *This Bridge Called My Back: Writings by Radical Women of Color.* New York: Kitchen Table.

Morris, Van Cleve. 1981. *Deaning: Middle Management in Academe.* Chicago: University of Illinois Press.

Murphy, Michael. 2000. "New Faculty for a New University: Toward a Full-Time Teaching-Intensive Faculty Track in Composition." *College Composition and Communication* 52: 14–42.

Murray, Piper. 2003. "'Containing Creatures We Barely Imagine': Responding to 'Bad' Students' Writing." In *A Way to Move*, edited by Jacobs and Micciche, 92–100. Portsmouth, NH: Boynton/Cook.

Myers-Breslin, Linda, ed. 1999. *Administrative Problem-Solving for Writing Programs and Writing Centers: Scenarios in Effective Program Management.* Urbana, IL: NCTE.

Nelson, Cary, ed. 1997. *Will Teach for Food.* Minneapolis: University of Minnesota Press.

Newkirk, Thomas. 2002. "Introduction." In *What to Expect When You're Expected to Teach,* edited by Bramblett and Knoblauch, 1–8.

Nias, Jennifer. 1996. "Thinking About Feeling: The Emotions in Teaching." *Cambridge Journal of Education* 26:293–306.

Nicholson, Linda J. 1990. *Feminism/Postmodernism.* New York: Routledge.

Niedenthal, Paula M., Lawrence W. Barsalou, François Ric, and Silvia Krauth-Gruber. 2005. "Embodiment in the Acquisition and Use of Emotion Knowledge." In *Emotion and Consciousness,* edited by Barrett et al., 21–50. New York: Guilford Press.

Noddings, Nel. 1996. "Stories and Affect in Teacher Education." *Cambridge Journal of Education* 26:435–47.

O'Dair, Sharon. 2000. "Stars, Tenure, and the Death of Ambition." In *Day Late, Dollar Short,* edited by Herman, 45–61. Albany, NY: SUNY Press.

Olson, Gary A. 1996. "Writing, Literacy and Technology: Toward a Cyborg Writing." *JAC* 16.1: 1–26.

———, and Joseph M. Moxley. 1989. "Directing Freshman Composition: The Limits of Authority." *College Composition and Communication* 40:51–59.

Parker, William Riley. 1988. "Where Do English Departments Come From?" In *The Writing Teacher's Sourcebook,* 2nd ed., edited by Gary Tate and Edward P.J. Corbett, 3–15. New York: Oxford University Press.

Payne, Michelle. 2000. *Bodily Discourses: When Students Write About Abuse and Eating Disorders.* Portsmouth, NH: Boynton/Cook.

Popken, Randall. 2004. "Edwin Hopkins and the Costly Labor of Composition Teaching." *College Composition and Communication* 55:618–41.

"'The Portland Resolution': Guidelines for Writing Program Administrator Positions." 1992. *WPA: Writing Program Administration* 16.1–2 (Fall/Winter):88–94

Powell, Malea. 2002. "Rhetorics of Survivance: How American Indians Use Writing." *College Composition and Communication* 53: 396–434.

Quandahl, Ellen. 2003. "A Feeling for Aristotle: Emotion in the Sphere of Ethics." In *A Way to Move,* edited by Jacobs and Micciche, 11–22. Portsmouth, NH: Boynton/Cook.

Reichert, Pegeen. 1996. "A Contributing Listener and Other Composition Wives: Reading and Writing the Feminine Metaphors in Composition Studies." *JAC* 16:141–57.

Rorty, Amélie. 1980. *Explaining Emotions*. Berkeley and Los Angeles: University of California Press.

Rose, Mike. 1989. *Lives on the Boundary: The Struggles and Achievements of America's Underprepared*. New York: The Free Press.

Rose, Shirley K., and Irwin Weiser, eds. 1999. *The Writing Program Administrator as Researcher: Inquiry in Action and Reflection*. Portsmouth, NH: Boynton/Cook.

Roskelly, Hephzibah, and David A. Jolliffe. 2005. *Everyday Use: Rhetoric at Work in Reading and Writing*. New York: Pearson Longman.

Roskelly, Hephzibah, and Kate Ronald. 1998. *Reason to Believe: Romanticism, Pragmatism, and the Possibility of Teaching*. Albany, NY: SUNY Press.

Royster, Jacqueline Jones. 2000. *Traces of a Stream: Literacy and Social Change Among African-American Women*. Pittsburgh, PA: University of Pittsburgh Press.

Rubin, Gayle. [1975] 1990. "The Traffic in Women: Notes on the 'Political Economy.'" In *Women, Class, and the Feminist Imagination: A Socialist-Feminist Reader*, edited by Karen V. Hansen and Ilene J. Philipson, 74–113. Philadelphia: Temple University Press.

Ruddick, Sara. 1984. "Maternal Thinking." In *Mothering: Essays in Feminist Theory*, edited by Joyce Trebilcot, 213–30. Totowa, NJ: Rowman.

Sarchett, Barry. 2000. "Introduction: Politics and Theory Redux." *ADE Bulletin* 126 (Fall):1–5. 24 May 2001 <http://www.ade.org/ade/bulletin/n126/126012.htm>.

Schechner, Richard. 1998. "What Is Performance Studies Anyway?" In *The Ends of Performance*, edited by Peggy Phelan and Jill Lane, 357–62. New York: New York University Press.

———. 2002. "Foreword: Fundamentals of Performance Studies." In *Teaching Performance Studies*, edited by Stucky and Wimmer, ix–xii. Carbondale, IL: SIUP.

———. 1998a. "The Costs of Caring: 'Femininism' and Contingent Women Workers in Composition Studies." In *Feminism and Composition Studies*, edited by Jarratt and Worsham, 74–93. New York: MLA.

Schell, Eileen E. 1992. "The Feminization of Composition: Questioning the Metaphors That Bind Women Teachers." *Composition Studies/Freshman English News* 20 (Spring): 55–61.

———. 1998b. *Gypsy Academics and Mother-Teachers: Gender, Contingent Labor, and Writing Instruction*. Portsmouth, NH: Boynton/Cook.

————, and Patricia Lambert Stock, eds. 2001. *Moving a Mountain: Transforming the Role of Contingent Faculty in Composition Studies and Higher Education.* Urbana, IL: NCTE.

Schuster, Charles I. 1991. "The Politics of Promotion." In *The Politics of Writing Instruction*, edited by Bullock and Trimbur, 85–95. Portsmouth, NH: Boynton/Cook.

————. 1995. "Foreword." In *Resituating Writing*, edited by Janangelo and Hansen, ix–xiv. Portsmouth, NH: Boynton/Cook.

Schutzman, Mady. 2006. "Ambulant Pedagogy." In *The Sage Handbook of Performance Studies*, edited by Madison and Hamera, 278–95. London: Sage.

Sirc, Geoffrey. 2001. "Review: The Schoolmaster in the Bookshelf." *College English* 63: 517–29.

Slevin, James F. 1991. "Depoliticizing and Politicizing Composition Studies." In *The Politics of Writing Instruction*, edited by Bullock and Trimbur, 1–21. Portsmouth, NH: Boynton/Cook.

Sommers, Shula. 1988. "Understanding Emotions: Some Interdisciplinary Considerations." In *Emotion and Social Change*, edited by Stearns and Stearns, 23–38. New York: Holmes & Meier.

Spelman, Elizabeth V. 1989. "Anger and Insubordination." In *Women, Knowledge, and Reality*, edited by Garry and Pearsall, 263–73. Boston: Unwin Hyman.

Stearns, Carol Zisowitz, and Peter N. Stearns, eds. 1988. *Emotion and Social Change: Toward a New Psychohistory.* New York: Holmes & Meier.

Stearns, Peter. 1986. "Anger and American Work: A Twentieth Century Turning Point." In *Anger: The Struggle for Emotional Control in American History*, edited by Carol Stearns and Peter Stearns, 123–48. Chicago: University of Chicago Press.

Strickland, Donna. 1998. "How to Compose a Capitalist." *Composition Forum* 9:25–38.

————. 2004. "The Managerial Unconscious of Composition Studies." In *Tenured Bosses and Disposable Teacher*, edited by Bousquet et al., 46–56. Carbondale, IL: SIUP.

Stucky, Nathan. 2002. "Deep Embodiment: The Epistemology of Natural Performance." In *Teaching Performance Studies*, edited by Stucky and Wimmer, 131–44. Carbondale, IL: SIUP.

————, and Cynthia Wimmer. 2002a. "Introduction: The Power of Transformation in Performance Studies Pedagogy." In *Teaching Performance Studies*, edited by Stucky and Wimmer, 1–29. Carbondale, IL: SIUP.

————, eds. 2002b. *Teaching Performance Studies.* Carbondale, IL: SIUP.

Syverson, Margaret A. 1999. *The Wealth of Reality: An Ecology of Composition*. Carbondale, IL: SIUP.

Tassoni, John, and William H. Thelin, eds. 2000. *Blundering for a Change: Errors and Expectations in Critical Pedagogy*. Portsmouth, NH: Boynton/Cook.

Terada, Rei. 2001. *Feeling in Theory: Emotion after the "Death of the Subject."* Cambridge, MA: Harvard University Press.

Tobin, Lad. 1991. "Reading Students, Reading Ourselves: Revising the Teacher's Role in the Writing Class." *College English* 53: 333–48.

Tompkins, Jane. 1991. "Me and My Shadow." In *Feminisms: An Anthology of Literary Theory and Criticism*, edited by Robyn R. Warhol and Diane Price Herndl, 1079–92. New Brunswick, NJ: Rutgers University Press.

———. 1996. *A Life in School: What the Teacher Learned*. Reading, MA: Addison-Wesley.

Tucker, Allan. 1992. *Chairing the Academic Department: Leadership Among Peers*, 3rd ed. New York: American Council on Education and MacMillan Publishing Company.

———, and Robert A. Bryan. 1991. *The Academic Dean: Dove, Dragon, and Diplomat*, 2nd ed. New York: American Council on Education and MacMillan Publishing Company.

Tuell, Cynthia. 1993. "Composition Teaching as 'Women's Work': Daughters, Handmaids, Whores, and Mothers." In *Writing Ourselves Into the Story*, edited by Fontaine and Hunter, 123–139. Carbondale, IL: SUIP.

Villanueva, Victor. 1993. *Bootstraps: From an American Academic of Color*. Urbana, IL: NCTE.

Walcott, Rinaldo. 1998. "Queer Texts and Performativity: Zora, Rap, and Community." In *Queer Theory in Education*, edited by William Pinar, 157–71. Mahwah, NJ: Lawrence Erlbaum Associates.

Walker, Jeffrey. 2000. *Rhetoric and Poetics in Antiquity*. New York: Oxford University Press.

Wapner, Paul. 2003. "Ecological Thinking: Studying Global Environmental Politics with a Wild Mind and a Mindful Heart." In *Encountering Global Environmental Politics: Teaching, Learning, and Empowering Knowledge*, edited by Michael Maniates, 17–33. New York: Rowman & Littlefield.

White, Edward M. 1991. "Use It or Lose It: Power and the WPA." *WPA: Writing Program Administration* 15.1–2:3–12.

Wiederhold, Eve. 2002. "The Face of Mourning: Deploying Grief to Construct a Nation." *JAC* 22:847–89.

Williams, Jeffrey. 1999. "Brave New University." *College English* 61: 742–51.

Williams, Joseph M. 2003. *Style: Ten Lessons in Clarity and Grace,* 7th ed. New York: Longman.

Winans, Amy. 2005. "Local Pedagogies and Race: Interrogating White Safety in the Rural College Classroom." *College English* 67:253–73.

———. 1998a. "After Words: A Choice of Words Remains." In *Feminism and Composition Studies,* edited by Jarratt and Worsham, 329–56. New York: MLA.

———. 2003. "Afterword." In *A Way to Move,* edited by Jacobs and Micciche, 161–63. Portsmouth, NH: Boynton/Cook.

———. 1998b. "Going Postal: Pedagogic Violence and the Schooling of Emotion." *JAC* 18.2:213–45.

Worsham, Lynn. 1991. "Writing against Writing: The Predicament of *Ecriture Féminine* in Composition Studies." In *Contending With Words: Composition and Rhetoric in a Postmodern Age,* edited by Patricia Harkin and John Schilb, 82–104. New York: MLA.

WPA Executive Committee. 1996. "Evaluating the Intellectual Work of Writing Program Administrators: A Draft." *WPA: Writing Program Administration* 20.1–2:92–103.

Yoon, K. Hyoejin. 2005. "Affecting the Transformative Intellectual: Questioning 'Noble' Sentiments in Critical Pedagogy and Composition." *JAC* 25.4:717–59.

Young, Morris. 2004. *Minor Re/Visions: Asian American Literacy Narratives as a Rhetoric of Citizenship.* Carbondale, IL: SIUP.

Zembylas, Michalinos. 2003. "Interrogating 'Teacher-Identity': Emotion, Resistance, and Self-Formation." *Educational Theory* 53:107–27.

Index